100

best

nonprofits

to

work for

100
best
nonprofits
to
work for

LESLIE HAMILTON
and ROBERT TRAGERT

Macmillan • USA

First Edition

Macmillan Reference USA
A Simon & Schuster Macmillan Company
1633 Broadway
New York, NY 10019-6785

An ARCO Book

ARCO is a registered trademark of Simon & Schuster Inc.
MACMILLAN is a registered trademark of Macmillan, Inc.

Manufactured in the United States of America

10 9 8 7 6 5 4 3 2 1

Library of Congress Number: 97-070018

ISBN: 0-02-861840-8

Dedication

To your career.

Acknowledgments

Our grateful thanks go out to: Elin Woodger, Ann Boder, Anna Botelho, and Bert Holtje, all of whom helped us to turn this book into a reality. Jennifer Perillo and Linda Bernbach showed both patience and vision in shepherding the book through its various stages. Judith Burros supplied invaluable fact-checking help and moral support throughout the process.

Table of Contents

INTRODUCTION

Is it possible that the era of looking for a good job with a stable, solid *company* has given way to the era of looking for a good job with a stable, solid *nonprofit*?

For many workers, the nonprofit sector has turned out to be the answer to any number of vexing career questions having to do with long-term career stability, competitive levels of compensation, and (last but not least) a sense of meaning and personal fulfillment on the job. During a period often marked by chaos and uncertainty in the private-sector workplace, nonprofit organizations as a whole have experienced surprising growth—even in the face of cutbacks in federal, state, and local funding. For an ever-larger number of job seekers, the familiar injunction to "do well by doing good" has been translated into the chance to work for good money at a nonprofit with a mission in which they can believe. At the same time, these workers have, in many cases, attained a greater measure of predictability in their career paths than that afforded by a previous employer.

What *is* a nonprofit organization? These entities exist in the realm between government and business. Their goal is to accomplish what businesses usually won't and governments usually can't. Typically, nonprofits strive to bring about some form of social change or improvement in an area that is outside the primary interest of a business, and too specialized (or too controversial) for the broad brush of government.

The word "nonprofit" is actually misleading, because it sometimes gives people the impression that the organization in question is capable of operating at a loss. It can't! The better phrase would be "non-*private*-profit." These entities have committed to operating, not for private benefit but with the aim of devoting every possible post-expense resource to their stated missions. Their efficiency in carrying out that goal is one of the main yardsticks by which their success is measured.

The nonprofit organization comes into play when a particular social goal is left unattended by business and government, and when enough people band together for the purpose of generating resources—turning a profit, if you will—that will be pointed toward the attainment of that social goal, rather than toward private gain. It is important to remember, however, that a nonprofit, like a business, must grow in order to survive. Once it stops growing, it starts dying.

A nonprofit organization exists to provide a service. It acts on a mandate from a specialized (and sometimes highly focused) segment of society. Its profits, while not its only reason for existing, *do* allow it to provide the service in question. Loss of either mandate or profit will spell the death of the organization.

The best nonprofits are run as efficiently as any successful business; at the same time, they are supremely dedicated to providing the service their supporters expect. This balancing act is an ongoing feature of a sector that offers some of the most challenging, demanding, and rewarding careers in our economy.

Our goal has been to identify the most desirable employers, large and small, in this exciting sector of the economy, to offer an idea of the guiding forces behind each, and thereby to give you an idea of the best ways to tie what you offer as a job applicant to what the organization in question is likely to need from its employees.

Here you will find one hundred top organizations of varying sizes. Each is recognized as among the leaders in its areas of activity. How were the organizations selected? Let's take a look at the process we followed in identifying companies for this book.

How We Chose the Organizations

There are over 700,000 nonprofit organizations in the United States, employing a total of nearly 10 million people. To pick the best nonprofits to work for *now*—the ones likeliest to offer jobs with meaningful current or future career potential, and to be able to sustain their current favorable positions in their respective operating areas, we tracked down the most recent information available. To be included in this book, an organization had to meet at least three out of four of the following standards:

Staff Size: No matter how stellar the organization, a small staff means comparatively few openings for those trying to get in the door, and reduced opportunity for advancement for those who eventually do. Organizations that employ fewer than a hundred employees were not considered to have met the staff size criteria.

Operating Budget: A one-million-dollar annual operating budget, we concluded, was an important dividing line between nonprofit operations. Some job seekers are most comfortable with the twin aims of staking out a competitive salary plan *and* working for an organization that pursues goals in accordance with their personal values. Our interviews with people in the nonprofit world led us to believe that nonprofits with an annual budget under one million dollars may face greater economic challenges, and offer significantly less career stability, than other nonprofits.

Years in Operation: To be considered as having met this standard, a nonprofit had to have been up and running for a minimum of three years.

Internal Mission Orientation: This is a subjective but vitally important standard measuring the institution's record of follow-through with regard to its stated purpose and its ability to impart a sense of that purpose to employees at all levels. The purpose of this standard is to assess the organization's ability to make an employee feel, even in an entry-level position, that he or she is contributing to the attainment of an important, identifiable organizational goal—a goal that is in consonance with important values and that is an integral part of the employer's reason for existence. Not all nonprofit organizations impart this feeling to the people who work for them. Accordingly, we used this standard to evaluate an operation's likelihood of making progress toward stated goals *by establishing a culture that is strongly linked to its mission*, and by propagating that culture at high and low levels alike.

We evaluated possible candidates against these four criteria by reviewing thousands of pages of data from nonprofits, discussing our selections with various nonprofit professionals, and reviewing the materials nonprofit organizations are required by law to file annually. The result is the 100 employers that make up the heart of this book. Each employer has been profiled in detail to aid you in your job search. We have included both established, well-known organizations where openings are highly competitive—and groups that seemed to us to represent excellent initial points of entry, perhaps through an internship, a volunteer assignment, or a modest initial job opportunity. An affiliation with a nonprofit in the latter category may well help you establish yourself down the road with one of the better-known outfits in the same general field.

Listing Analysis

Each entry features the following elements:

Overview: This provides you with a summary of the nonprofit's operations.

By the Numbers: This offers budgeting and staff data in those cases where recent information was available to us in these areas. In many cases, this part of the listing also offers us a look at some critical operating figures that may provide insight into the group's accomplishments over time. Please remember that nonprofits, like any other employers, are subject to change. Use the figures in this part of the book to develop a good working knowledge of the organization in question, not to form final judgments on the precise current size or scope of a program or group.

The Mission: Here you'll find out about the guiding objectives of the nonprofit—important information if you plan to approach the group about employment, volunteer, or internship opportunities.

Words to the Wise: This part of the entry offers the best information we were able to uncover on finding work with the organization in question.

What to Expect: This tells you what's on the horizon for the group in question—and the people who work for it.

Potent Quote: This is an invaluable verbatim quote by or about the group in question. It will usually shed some light on the way the organization's leadership views the challenges and the opportunities it now faces. This part of the entry often gives you important information about recent initiatives or shifts in historic orientation, information you should probably familiarize yourself with before any job interview.

"Which Is the Right Nonprofit For Me?"

The real question is: Which nonprofit are you right for?

All the nonprofits in this book represent excellent employment opportunities. By the same token, each possesses a unique culture and work environment, and each must be approached on its own merits, with a firm understanding of the organization's goals. While it is certainly true that a private-sector job search is likeliest to be successful when it incorporates a good deal of early research on each prospective employer, the research you conduct before contacting a *nonprofit* employer is probably even more important. Why? These employers are looking not only for a set of skills but also for a particular type of person: someone who can demonstrate a unique passion for the organization's stated social goal.

If you approach one of the employers in this book without a true passion for the organization's mission—and by that we mean its purpose, its chosen means of trying to make the world a better place—and focus exclusively on your personal goals, or on issues of efficiency and compensation, you'll be missing half of the equation. Yes, you should certainly be able to deliver results in your field of expertise, and yes, you deserve to be compensated fairly for your efforts. Bear in mind, however, that many of the people with whom you will be working are there not simply because they hope to move ahead in their careers, but because they believe deeply in the cause to which they are devoting their working hours.

If your personal philosophy doesn't match up with that of the target organization, there's not much chance of things turning out well for you or the employer. When identifying companies in this book to target for employment appeals, remember that the core values that guide you should play as large a role in your selection process as issues related to compensation, relocation, and advancement. It's an excellent bet that you will never be able to change the nonprofit's view of *its* stated mission—and if it turns out that your social views differ radically from that of the organization, its attempt to change you (or its decision that it's time to part company) may be unpleasant for all concerned.

Every nonprofit has its own unique aim, its own way of looking at the world. Does your personal style fit within that aim and that culture?

Your ability to answer that question honestly will have a great deal to do with your long-term success in the nonprofit sector.

Other Tools in This Book

This book also offers a summary of the best job search advice. See Appendix A for a concise review of the successful person-to-person job search campaign in the private sector, as well as valuable advice on developing your customized resume and making the most of your cover letter.

In Appendix B you'll find a listing of employment resources. In Appendix C you'll find an index of the 100 nonprofits by field of operation.

Tell Us What You Think!

We're eager to hear your feedback on this book. If you have questions, comments, or suggestions on how to make future editions better, write to us! Here's the address:

Robert Tragert and Leslie Hamilton
c/o ARCO Books
1633 Broadway, 7th Floor
New York, NY 10019

The 100 Best Nonprofits to Work for

AIDS Project—Los Angeles

1313 N. Vine Street, Los Angeles, California, 90028
213/993-1600
World Wide Web: http://www.apla.org/apla/
Contact: Jeanie Minty

Overview

With a client base of over 4,000 and a powerful lobbying organization, Aids Project—Los Angeles (APLA) does a superior job of raising awareness of HIV and AIDS and bringing about legislation to improve care and services for HIV/AIDS patients. Founded in 1983, the organization has made great strides in obtaining government funding for HIV prevention and education programs, ensuring the availability of health insurance and Medi-Cal benefits for people with HIV, defeating legislation that would have eliminated anonymous testing and required the reporting of HIV-positive names, and protecting AIDS-based care centers and hospitals from budget cuts that would have forced them to close. The organization boasts numerous other accomplishments for its service group. It is recognized as a national leader in the AIDS movement.

By the Numbers

Staff: 220.

Budget: $19,000,000.

Individual contributions make up 76 percent of APLA's funding. Direct mail brings in 6 percent; the remainder is derived from other sources.

The Mission

APLA provides services and information to people in Los Angeles County who are afflicted with or interested in knowing more about

HIV/AIDS. Firmly committed to community needs, the organization also serves as an advocate for people with HIV/AIDS in local, county, state, and federal governments. In addition to providing basic assistance and services to people with HIV or at risk for HIV, APLA works with other organizations to reduce the incidence of HIV infection. Through a combination of lobbying, publishing, organizing human services within the community, public education, and training and technical programs, the organization strives to make a critical impact on HIV/AIDS prevention and management.

Words to the Wise

On average, there are 30 staff openings per year. The majority of paid employees are either caseworkers or office managers/support staff. Thus, a degree in social work or strong office skills may provide the best points of entry. Fundraising experience is also a plus. A limited number of interns are accepted on a volunteer basis for college credit. In fact, the best entry to APLA may be through volunteerism. The organization relies heavily on over 2,500 volunteers, far outnumbering its paid staff. Proven dedication to APLA's goals and experience in working with HIV-affected clients may be the best gateway to paid employment within the organization.

What to Expect

The APLA currently provides direct services to thousands of people and educates thousands more through its Hotline, media campaigns, advocacy efforts, and special programs aimed at raising the quality of life for people living with HIV or AIDS. It has entered into partnership with numerous other organizations to enable the provision of community-based services, technical support, and financial assistance to all who need it. The organization is understandably proud of its accomplishments. It will continue to build on them, but looks to the day when a cure for AIDS is discovered and its services will no longer be needed.

HIV infection and AIDS are two of the most prevalent medical and social issues in the country today. Work for APLA will aid in current efforts to stop the spread of misinformation about the disease and prejudice against HIV/AIDS-infected patients. In addition, as improved treatments become available, improvements can also be made in the quality of services provided to the community. Employment with APLA should therefore provide a rich sense of moral satisfaction. Bear in mind, however, that this field can be emotionally draining, especially for those who provide direct care to clients. There can also be frustration if desired legislation does not pass or efforts fail to halt laws that discriminate against the group APLA serves. Be prepared to work long hours. The dedication required in APLA work often calls for putting in time far beyond the normal forty-hour work week.

Potent Quote

"APLA is a resource for persons falling within the full spectrum of HIV. APLA adapts as necessary to the changing course of the pandemic. APLA aims for sensitivity and competence in providing services to its diverse client base. APLA's programs and services are driven by client need. APLA primarily addresses the common needs of HIV seropositive clients and the needs of persons at risk for HIV disease. APLA's services are determined by the degree to which APLA can make a critical impact. APLA is part of a broader, comprehensive system of HIV prevention, medical care, and support services. APLA is committed to working in collaboration and partnership with other organizations for the benefit of people with HIV to manage their illness to the maximum extent possible."

(From the organization's mission statement.)

Alcoholics Anonymous World Services

> *475 Riverside Drive, New York, New York 10163*
> *212/870-3400*
> *Fax: 212/870-3003*
> *World Wide Web: http://www.alcoholics-anonymous.org/*
> *Contact: Lois Fisher.*
> *"Committee reviews resumes and narrows submissions down*
> *to a manageable number; then interviews are set up."*

Overview

Founded in 1935, Alcoholics Anonymous (A.A.) is an organization of over two million recovering alcoholics in the U.S. and other countries. Not associated with any religious, political, or ethnic organization or sect, the organization has earned considerable success and applause through the years for its outstanding work in helping alcoholics achieve sobriety.

By the Numbers

A.A. is entirely self-supporting, thanks to member contributions and sales from books and literature. The organization does not seek or accept contributions from non-members, and limits voluntary contributions from members to $1,000 or less on an annual basis. There are no fees or dues for joining A.A., nor are there any governing officers, rules, or regulations. A limited organizational structure operates through two corporations. A.A. World Services consists of approximately eighty-four workers who keep A.A. groups in touch domestically and internationally and field inquiries regarding A.A. programs and groups, and who also prepare, publish and distribute A.A. literature. **A.A. Grapevine, Inc.** publishes the organization's monthly international journal, *A.A. Grapevine*, along with cassette tapes, anthologies, and other materials. Both A.A. World Services and A.A. Grapevine, Inc. report to the General Service Board of A.A., a board of trustees consisting of fourteen A.A. members and seven non-alcoholic friends of the A.A. Fellowship.

The trustees meets once a year in a General Service Conference, which is also attended by directors and staff from the General Service Office and the Grapevine, as well as ninety-two delegates from A.A. areas in the United States and Canada. This conference provides an operating link among the various groups. On a local level, formal organization is kept to a minimum, generally with a steering committee and a rotating set of officers.

The Mission
A.A. brings together people with a common problem, alcoholism, to solve that problem and to help others become sober. Their primary tool is a 12-step program that involves sharing experiences, strength, and hope in a spirit of fellowship. The guiding principle of A.A. is that alcoholism is a disease for which the only answer is abstinence from drink. The only requisite for joining is a desire to stop drinking.

A prominent spiritual component has historically been embodied within many of the organization's teachings.

Words to the Wise
Questions on professional employment opportunities may be forwarded to the New York office.

What to Expect
A.A. is currently undergoing a period of change as it seeks the best ways to serve its constituency. Originally begun as a haven and support group for people with drinking problems, it has increasingly been attracting younger people with drug addictions and emotional trauma. Many are sent to A.A. under court order as part of their sentence for a criminal conviction. This has led to a significant gap between generations of members, and a conflict regarding the goals of the organization and whether it should try to be so all-encompassing. Nevertheless, with nearly two million members worldwide, the organization remains a vitally important—some might say towering—feature in the landscape of alcohol abuse treatment programs.

Potent Quote

"A.A. had its beginnings in 1935 at Akron, Ohio, as the outcome of a meeting between Bill W., a New York stockbroker, and Dr. Bob S., an Akron surgeon. Both had been hopeless alcoholics. Prior to that time, Bill and Dr. Bob had each been in contact with the Oxford Group, a mostly nonalcoholic fellowship that emphasized universal spiritual values in daily living. In that period, the Oxford Groups in America were headed by the noted Episcopal clergyman, Dr. Samuel Shoemaker. Under this spiritual influence, and with the help of an old-time friend, Ebby T., Bill had gotten sober and then maintained his recovery by working with other alcoholics, though none of these had actually recovered. Meanwhile, Dr. Bob's Oxford Group membership at Akron had not helped him enough to achieve sobriety. When Dr. Bob and Bill finally met, the effect on the doctor was immediate. This time, he found himself face to face with a fellow sufferer who had made good.... [He] soon got sober, never to drink again. The founding spark of A.A. had been struck."

(From *The Birth of A.A. and Its Growth in U.S./Canada.*)

American Association of Retired Persons

> *601 E Street, NW, Washington, D.C. 20049*
> *202/434-2828 (Job line)*
> *World Wide Web: http://www.aarp.org/*
> *Contact: Job line number above*

Overview

The American Association of Retired Persons (AARP) has gained a reputation as the most influential lobby in Washington, as well as one of the most potent forces active in the formation of legislation on behalf of the elderly and the retired. Its membership is ten times the size of the National Rifle Association; among U.S. nonprofit groups, it is surpassed only by the Catholic Church in overall size. Membership is open to persons fifty and older.

By the Numbers

Staff: 1,800.

Budget: $359,700,000 in total operating expenses.

With a membership base of over 33 million (approximately 20 percent of all registered voters), the organization maintains offices in 21 states and a volunteer force of 200,000 throughout the country. Its headquarters in Washington includes a think tank of thirty-two scholars and nineteen staff lobbyists.

AARP was formed in 1958 with funding from the proceeds of health insurance sales to individuals sixty-five and older. Health insurance continues to provide the largest source of income for the organization, in addition to offerings such as annuities and prescription drugs. The association also earns income through mutual funds, auto rentals, automobile club memberships, affinity Visa and MasterCard sales, and hotel discount packages. As a result of these revenue sources, basic membership in the AARP is only $8.00 per year.

The Mission

A membership organization devoted to the concerns and standard of living of people aged fifty and older, the AARP works to enhance the quality of life by promoting independence, dignity, and a sense of purpose through educational and advocacy services. Their publication *Modern Maturity* (published six times a year) has the largest circulation of any periodical in the nation. The AARP describes its goal as to "improve every aspect of living for older people."

Words to the Wise

The AARP is so large that it provides numerous entry-level positions in its different offices. For some of these jobs, marketing experience is a plus. Many job openings are advertised in newspapers or through other channels.

The AARP is headed by Horace B. Deets, a widely respected figure considered to be a major player in Washington politics. Under Deets's leadership, AARP continues to exercise significant influence over the national political agenda. He has also done much to broaden the focus of the AARP from advisory and advocacy services for the older population to activities catering to the (comparatively) younger, not-yet-retired population. AARP members can now obtain airline discounts, car rental discounts, hotel and motel discounts, and insurance of all sorts, along with access to such services as a credit union, investment program, pharmacy discounts, and a travel agency that provides package tours.

A wide range of job opportunities exists within the organization.

What to Expect

AARP has engaged in numerous major initiatives over the years, including campaigns in health care improvements, worker equity, women's issues, and minority affairs. Advocacy efforts have included voting registration campaigns, medical and long-term care reform, a peer review program for hospitals and medical organizations, a utility intervention project, and lobbying efforts on the state and federal levels. While continuing to work in these areas, AARP will also be expanding its attempt to reach out to younger, still-working groups. The organization's leaders must decide how to prioritize its goals for each portion of its membership base. There is some question of whether comparatively younger and more independent members of the population will associate the group with stereotypes about the elderly. To combat this attitude, AARP's publications and products have already swung their emphasis to better cater to the needs and desires of nonretired members. The organization's leaders must also come to terms with the need for reforms in Medicare and Social Security, as aging baby boomers show increasing unwillingness to foot the bill for a troubled system that is unlikely to provide benefits for them when they reach retirement age.

Potent Quote:

"Size didn't save the dinosaurs."

(Horace B. Deets, Executive Director.)

American Civil Liberties Union

125 Broad Street, New York, New York 10004-2400
212/549-2500
World Wide Web: http://www.aclu.org/
Contact: Linda Gustafson, Office Administration
("for applicants other than attorneys")

Overview

The American Civil Liberties Union (ACLU) has been a part of the American legal landscape since 1920. The ACLU was set up to provide legal avenues for individual citizens to pursue when their legal rights had been trampled on. The first public-interest law firm of its kind, it exerts a powerful influence on the American legal system to this day. The ACLU's most publicized cases are probably those in which the organization seeks to defend the rights of individuals to free speech, equal protection of the law, due process, and the right to privacy. The ACLU has become the most widely recognized and influential advocate for individual rights in the nation. It is America's largest public-interest law firm.

By the Numbers

The ACLU is financially supported by membership fees and contributions from its more than 275,000 members, as well as from foundations and corporate donations. No government funding is accepted. The organizations is a "fifty-state network of staffed affiliate offices, more than 300 chapters in smaller towns, and regional offices in Denver and Atlanta." Over 60 staff attorneys work with approximately 2,000 volunteer attorneys, handling approximately 6,000 cases per year. The organization is governed by an 84-member Board of Directors. Each affiliate office is autonomous, but the various offices "collaborate" with the national office to attain shared objectives.

The Mission

The ACLU views itself as a guardian of the Bill of Rights, the first ten Amendments to the United States Constitution. The organization works to ensure that the fundamental freedoms guaranteed by the Bill of Rights are protected and preserved for future generations. ACLU leaders are careful to distinguish the Bill of Rights from the Constitution, which authorizes the government to act. The function of the Bill of Rights is to limit that authority. The ACLU takes as its mission the goal of ensuring that legal rights guaranteed by the Bill of Rights are upheld and not abused by the government. It has focused its attention on such areas as arts censorship, capital punishment, immigrants' rights, privacy and technology, reproductive freedom, women's rights, and workplace rights.

Words to the Wise

Despite its high profile and the polarizing nature of the cases it some-times selects, the ACLU explicitly denies any political agenda, and does not see itself as a partisan entity. Appeals to a particular social or polit-ical agenda run counter to the group's founding ideas, which position the group as devoted "exclusively to protecting the basic civil liberties of all Americans."

What to Expect

Expect challenging (and demanding) legal and support work pursued for its own sake.

The group emphasizes volunteer contributions and action. If you do not believe fervently in the goals and mission of the ACLU, there's not much point in volunteering or applying for work there.

Employment appeals to local affiliates may be more effective than those made to the national office; ask for a copy of the affiliate directory, or see the organization's web site.

Potent Quote

"When Roger Baldwin founded the ACLU in 1920, civil liberties were in a sorry state. Citizens were sitting in jail for holding antiwar views. U.S. Attorney General Palmer was conducting raids upon aliens holding unorthodox opinions. Racial segregation was the law of the land, and violence against blacks was routine. Sex discrimination was firmly institutionalized; it wasn't until 1920 that women even got the vote. Constitutional rights for homosexuals, the poor, prisoners, mental patients, and other special groups were literally unthinkable. And, perhaps most significantly, the Supreme Court had yet to uphold a single free speech claim under the First Amendment."

(From *A Brief History*.)

American Foundation for the Blind

11 Penn Plaza, Suite 300, New York, New York 10001
212/502-7600
World Wide Web: http://www.afb.org/afb/
Contact: Lesa Booth

Overview

Founded in 1921, the American Foundation for the Blind (AFB) is a renowned organization once championed by Helen Keller. It serves as a national resource for the blind and visually impaired as well as the public at large. The AFB achieves its goals through a combination of lobbying, public education, research, and a wide variety of publications and audio materials (i.e., Talking Books). It also provides training and technical assistance to those who need it, as well as services for other agencies (and individuals) that seek to employ, assist, and otherwise improve the quality of life for the visually impaired.

By the Numbers

Staff: Approximately 100.

Budget: $12,000,000.

Funding for the AFB comes from charitable foundations, direct-mail campaigns, and individual contributions. Its income is primarily spent on programs and services (publishing, information dissemination, consulting, and other services, a total of 71 percent of income), with the remainder divided among fund-raising efforts and administrative expenses (14 percent each).

The Mission

The AFB seeks to assist the blind and visually impaired in ways that promote independence and ensure equality of access, opportunities for all, and freedom of personal choice. The organization works to fulfill its mission in four primary areas of activity: (1) the development, collection, and dissemination of information regarding blindness and visual impairment; (2) the identification and analysis of critical issues, as well as attempts to resolve these issues; (3) the education of the public and government officials as the needs and capabilities of the blind and visually impaired; and (4) the production and distribution of audio materials for the blind.

The AFB responds to over 100,000 inquiries yearly "from people who are blind or visually impaired, their families and friends, professionals in the blindness field, and the general public."

Words to the Wise

The AFB has attracted a dedicated staff in which there is little turnover. On average, there are only a few job openings per year. The staff includes writers and editors, lawyers, office workers, accountants, fund-raisers, and lobbyists. Interns are occasionally taken on without pay. The AFB welcomes volunteers, which may be the best way to get a foot in the door.

Not long ago, the organization moved into new headquarters in New York City. It also maintains offices in San Francisco, Chicago, Atlanta, and Washington, D.C. After going through a period of significant downsizing (1992-1994), which could not have had a positive effect on morale, the AFB is now rebounding impressively. Despite the setbacks caused by downsizing, these changes ultimately fostered a better level of communication among employees. There is a strong commitment to the AFB's goals that provides a strong sense of unity and teamwork among the staff.

What to Expect

Efforts will continue to provide top-grade services and resources for the visually impaired. Recent projects and accomplishments have included the Blind Deaf-Blind Project, which resulted in Hand in Hand, a program focusing on the education of deaf-blind students to achieve better communication, mobility, and orientation in the seeing world; and a Braille Mentor Program, consisting of a series of workshops designed to train teacher-mentors and provide funds for developing in-service and local training in Braille. These and other programs to improve accessibility and educational needs, institute health care reform, and address a multitude of concerns for their constituency will continue to provide the primary focus for the AFB staff.

Potent Quote

"A nonprofit organization founded in 1921 and recognized as Helen Keller's cause in the United States, the American Foundation for the Blind is a leading national resource for people who are blind or visually impaired, the organizations that serve them, and the general public. The mission of the American Foundation for the Blind is to enable people who are blind or visually impaired to achieve equality of access and opportunity that will ensure freedom of choice in their lives."

(From the organization's web site.)

American Lung Association

1740 Broadway, New York, New York 10019-4374
212/315-8700
World Wide Web: http://www.lungusa.org/
Contact: Ruth Porter (address above), or Executive Director of local Association

Overview

As its name implies, the American Lung Association is dedicated to the promotion of healthy lungs and the conquest of lung disease. Specifically, the Association seeks to improve lung disease awareness and to provide public education about such issues as smoking and health. Much of this work is carried out by local Associations, which develop publications and community or family-based programs to achieve the desired goals of the ALA. There are Lung Associations in all fifty states, along with the District of Columbia, Puerto Rico, and the Virgin Islands. Publications include *American Journal of Respiratory and Critical Care Medicine* and *American Journal of Respiratory Cell and Molecular Biology*. The ALA also works in association with the American Thoracic Society.

By the Numbers

Staff: 175 in the New York office; up to 1,500 nationwide.

Budget: $120,000,000.

Each local Association is separately incorporated. Depending on the location and size of the individual Association, the budget can range from under $200,000 to over $2 million. Approximately 71 percent of a typical budget is spent on educational programs and community services, with the remainder allocated to fund raising (about 16 percent of budget), and administrative and other costs (13 percent).

The Mission

The American Lung Association seeks to prevent lung disease and promote lung health. The Association especially targets major issues of public concern: smoking and tobacco, air pollution, tuberculosis, asthma, and AIDS.

Words to the Wise

Contact the national office or check your local phone directory for information on the local Association near you. There are numerous opportunities for employment within the ALA. In addition to standard office and accounting openings, the organization employs writers and editors, fund raisers, and specialists in such areas as health education and communications. Part-time and summer employees, volunteers, and interns are all accepted. Jobs are advertised in local newspapers and posted at colleges. In addition, positions for specialists are frequently recruited through professional societies.

What to Expect

This organization is experiencing increasing visibility as our society focuses with greater intensity on the dangers associated with cigarette smoking. The American Lung Association is one of the nation's most important advocacy organizations on issues related to smoking and indoor air pollution related to cigarette smoke.

Potent Quote

"Local Lung Associations are separately incorporated; each handles its own recruiting and hiring work."

(National office spokesperson.
The headquarters office can supply
information on the Association nearest you.)

American Red Cross

8111 Gatehouse Road, 3rd Floor, Falls Church, Virginia 22042
703/206-6006 (Job line)
Fax: 703/206-8143
World Wide Web: http://www.redcross.org/
Contact: Human Resources Administration

Overview

The American Red Cross (ARC) is one of the largest humanitarian organizations in the United States, with over one million volunteers devoted to its mission. These volunteers have provided crucial services in times of emergency on both a national and an international level. This has included disaster planning, preparedness, education, and relief; emergency communications and assistance to members of the Armed Forces and their families; assistance with international disaster relief and preparedness, as well as tracing of victims and support for international humanitarian law; health and safety services, including courses in CPR, first aid, water safety, mission-related caregiving, and HIV/AIDS education; the distribution of blood, blood products, and tissue services; and maintenance of a National Office of Volunteers. The ARC enjoys a well-deserved reputation for being one of the most effective and reliable providers of humanitarian aid in the world.

By the Numbers

Staff: 32,262 paid staff; 1.39 million volunteers.

Budget: $1,800,000,000

The American Red Cross depends on generous contributions, primarily from individuals, for its continued support. Of the funds it receives, 92 percent goes into programs and services.

The Mission

The mission of the American Red Cross is to provide relief to victims of natural and man-made disasters, and to help people prepare for and respond to emergencies. It is guided in its mission by principles established in its Congressional Charter and the Fundamental Principles of the International Red Cross and Red Crescent Movement. These emphasize the organization's voluntary character and its dependence upon volunteers.

Words to the Wise

The best way into the ARC is by starting out as a volunteer. The organization provides training for most volunteer positions and looks for volunteers to serve in a variety of capacities, including governance, management, direct service (i.e., disaster relief and health and safety education), and advisory roles. For paid positions, opportunities are available on national and on regional levels in areas ranging from corporate to biomedical services. Information on career opportunities may be accessed at the ARC's web site.

What to Expect

The Red Cross provides crucial services to more than 14 million people annually. The organization is largely dependent on volunteers, who outnumber paid staff by a ratio of approximately 43 to 1. The ARC is overseen by a fifty-member Board of Governors, also consisting of volunteers, which sets national Red Cross policies. On both the national and the regional levels, the volunteer leadership maintains authority over the paid staff, from clerks to the organization's president. The ARC is keenly aware of the need to keep younger people involved in its activities in order to be more responsive to the changing world. To this end, their National Office of Volunteers is working to attract, involve, and develop a diverse, intergenerational work force. The resulting combination of dynamism and continuity strengthens the organization and guarantees its survival as its important and well respected work continues.

Potent Quote

"The Red Cross processes 4,000 emergency communications every day—one every 22 seconds. In 1995, the Red Cross oversaw 800,000 cases of assistance to members of the Armed Forces, civilians, and their families.... In 1995, the American Red Cross International Services worked with the International Red Cross and the Red Crescent Movement in some 170 nations around the world to provide relief and humanitarian assistance to those in need."

(From the organization's web site.)

American Rivers

801 Pennsylvania Avenue SE, Suite 400, Washington, D.C. 20003
202/547-6900
World Wide Web: http://www.amrivers.org/
Contact: Walter Sisson

Overview
American Rivers was founded in 1973 with the aim of expanding the number of rivers included in the National Wild and Scenic Rivers System. The organization promotes conservation and protection by working with local river activists, pursuing litigation, lobbying, and overseeing educational projects.

By the Numbers
Membership: Over 50,000.

Budget: $2,400,000.

Most of the organization's funding is provided by individuals and corporate contributors; a smaller amount comes from conference exposure, telephone solicitation, and direct mail. The organization has successfully lobbied for protection of 22,000 miles of riverways and 5.5 million acres of riverside land.

The Mission
The group works with federal, state, and tribal agencies to restore riverways and encourage an attitude of stewardship toward our country's rivers.

Words to the Wise

Only a few staff positions open in an average year. The organization employs attorneys, issue experts, fund raisers, clerical staff, writers, lobbyists, managers, and researchers. An internship program provides three-month assignments with a living stipend.

As of this writing, internship and employment opportunities are listed on the organization's web site.

What to Expect

The organization's blend of legislative research and action, grassroots organizing, and action to bring their work to the attention of media and government is likely to lead it to play an important role in environmental circles for some years to come.

Potent Quote

"American Rivers promotes public awareness about the importance of healthy rivers and the threats they face. Join our team as we develop scientifically sound and economically viable solutions to the challenges facing America's rivers in the 21st century."

(From the organization's web site.)

American Social Health Organization

> *P.O. Box 13827, Research Triangle Park, NC 27709*
> *Job Line: 919/361-4804*
> *Contact: Job Line*

Overview

The American Social Health Association (ASHA) has been in existence for over 80 years and holds the distinction of being the only independent national nonprofit organization dedicated to the prevention of sexually transmitted diseases (STDs). Founded in 1914 following an epidemic of venereal disease, ASHA devotes the greatest portion of its efforts to public education through brochures and other informational materials, and by the maintenance of confidential Hotlines that process 1.5 million calls every year. ASHA also publishes three quarterly newsletters and concentrates on advocacy and lobbying efforts to obtain governmental funding of STD programs at the local, state, and federal levels. The association sponsors a program that provides training and technical assistance for scientists entering the area of STD research. In addition, ASHA acts as the administrative agency for the National Coalition to Fight STDs. Recent initiatives include the formation of the Women's Health Program and a program entitled "Finding the Words."

By the Numbers

Staff: 100 full-time; 206 part-time.

Budget: $8,856,000.

The federal government provides 90 percent of ASHA's funding. The remainder is derived from individual contributions and foundations.

The Mission

ASHA seeks to put an end to sexually transmitted diseases and to educate communities, families, and individuals about such diseases and their harmful effects. Originally founded to combat venereal disease, ASHA developed a social awareness over the years that led it to expand its mission in the 1950s and 1960s to include the introduction of family life education into public school curricula and to fight drug abuse.

Words to the Wise

There may be up to twelve staff openings per year at salaries ranging from $22,000 to $31,000 annually, depending on position and college degree. Most of these openings are in administrative support and office positions. Less easy to access are the more specialized jobs of writers, editors, lobbyists, fund-raisers, technicians, and issue experts. No interns or summer employees are accepted, and there is a limited number of volunteers. ASHA employs a greater number of people in part-time than in full-time positions. Thus, a willingness to start as a part-timer may be the best way to gain full-time employment. Fluency in both Spanish and English could also offer an advantage, since many positions require a bilingual capability.

A recent trip to the organization's web site yielded detailed information about a number of open positions at various levels.

What to Expect

ASHA has served as the nation's conscience on the issue of STDs for over eighty years. As such, it has frequently had to change, adapt, and sometimes expand the methods of its operation to suit the changing times. However, the association's goals to eradicate sexually transmitted disease by providing honest and concise information and promoting open discussion have never changed and are likely to be relevant for years to come. The agency is active, well funded, and firmly committed to its mission.

Potent Quote

"ASHA operates the National AIDS Hotline and the National STD Hotline, the latter of which ASHA started as a volunteer program in 1979. (These programs are operated through a contract with the Centers for Disease Control and Prevention.) ASHA's privately funded programs include the Herpes Resource Center and National Herpes Hotline, the HPV (human papillomavirus) Support Program, the advocacy program, research program, and major programs in publications and media relations. ASHA also recently established a new program in the area of women's health. In confronting today's epidemic of STDs, ASHA draws on eight decades of experience as the country's main provider of STD services in education, research, and public policy."

(*Southern Medical Journal*, April 1995.)

Amnesty International, USA

> *322 Eighth Avenue, Tenth Floor, New York, New York 10001*
> *212/807-8400*
> *World Wide Web: http://www.amnesty.org/*
> *Contact: Human Resources*

Overview

Amnesty International (AI) is the driving force behind a worldwide human rights movement on behalf of prisoners of conscience. Formed in 1961 by British lawyer Peter Benenson, it is not associated with any particular government, political affiliation, or religious institution. The organization has investigated and publicized cases in many countries involving several categories of prisoners: prisoners of conscience; those who have been imprisoned without benefit of trial; prisoners subjected to torture and other cruel or degrading treatment or punishment; and political killings and "disappearances." AI also works to provide relief to refugees from dictatorial governments and political systems, and lobbies strenuously against the death penalty. It is an organization well known for its strong values and commitment to its goals of protecting all victims, regardless of their ideology or beliefs. In 1977, AI received a Nobel prize for its work, which continues to receive worldwide attention.

By the Numbers

Staff: 170 full and part time.

Budget: $22,000,000.

AI principles do not allow for any government support. Instead, it relies on membership fees and public contributions to support its work. More than 80 percent of Amnesty International's funding is obtained through direct-mail campaigns. The remainder is provided through contributions from individuals, foundations, and other sources. In the mid-1980s, a number of prominent musicians and artists adopted AI as a personal cause. The resulting publicity generated increased contributions and growth, with a corresponding increase in AI's budget and its ability to open new offices and hire new staff. The majority of the organization's budget is allocated to programs and services, with the remainder going toward fund-raising and administrative expenses.

The Mission

Amnesty International is an independent organization dedicated to assisting and working for the release of all persons imprisoned, detained, or restricted access because of their political or religious beliefs or because of their ethnicity, color, language, or sex. It also works for quick and fair trials for such individuals. With over 400,000 members in the USA organized into local and campus groups, AI seeks to achieve its goals through a combination of public education and organizing on a community level, along with multi-media publicity and the collection and dissemination of information on human rights violations. In this way, the organization has built a general public awareness of and support for its concerns and work. AI also generates numerous reports and newsletters targeted for certain segments of the world's population in an effort to increase awareness among specific groups. The fundamental belief that guides AI in its work is that the protection of human rights is an international responsibility.

Words to the Wise

There can be anywhere from six to ten staff openings on a yearly basis, with no one area appearing to be stronger than any other. Jobs are advertised in newspapers and AI publications, as well as through college placement offices and word of mouth. AI also relies heavily on volunteers to carry out large portions of its work, including letter-writing campaigns, staffing tables at public events, and organizing public demonstrations. AI employs direct-mail professionals, fund raisers, writers, accountants, press aides, and administrative and office professionals.

What to Expect

Although it has occasionally come under attack for some of the causes it has championed and some of the methods it has used, AI is generally lauded for its effectiveness, accuracy, and impartiality. The organization has established a reputation as a respected and credible source of information on human rights throughout the world, and it works vigilantly to maintain its independence from all governmental, political, religious, and economic influences. AI never claims credit for the release of prisoners, which is often the result of many factors, but the group's work nevertheless plays a major role in the international human rights movement. With the admiration and support of numerous prominent and influential people, it is likely that AI will continue to grow and expand its efforts through the coming years.

Potent Quote

"Amnesty International has more than 1,000,000 members, subscribers, and regular donors in more than 100 countries and territories and 4,287 local Amnesty International groups... There are nationally organized sections in 54 countries, 33 of them in Latin America and the Caribbean, Africa, Asia, and the Middle East and Central Europe. The organization's nerve center is the International Secretariat in London, with more than 300 permanent staff and 95 volunteers form more than fifty countries."

(From the organization's web site.)

Beth Israel Deaconess Medical Center

330 Brookline Avenue, Boston MA 02215
617/632-9400
World Wide Web: http://www.bidmc.harvard.edu/
Contact: Human Resources

Overview

Established in 1916, the Beth Israel Corporation recently merged with the New England Deaconess Hospital to form the Beth Israel Deaconess Medical Center, the center of a regional system of health maintenance for both in-patients and out-patients. With 371 adult beds, more than 29,800 patient admissions each year, and over 41,000 visits annually in their 24-hour emergency room, the organization is one of the largest and most reputable providers of health care in the country. The hospital also maintains a general medical facility for ambulatory care (BI Healthcare Associates); specialty units for outpatients logging over 183,000 visits annually; and a home care program for homebound patients who are acutely or chronically ill, providing teams of physicians, nurse practitioners, and social workers making over 35,000 visits per year. The institution is also a teaching hospital affiliated with Harvard Medical School and operates numerous clinics and health care facilities throughout the metropolitan Boston area.

By the Numbers

Staff: Approximately 1,800 locally.

Annual revenues: Approximately $436 million.

The Mission

The institution's focus is to provide high-quality health care for patients.

Words to the Wise

In addition to a professional staff of physicians and nurses, the hospital offers career opportunities for accountants, secretaries, and program operators. Jobs are advertised in newspapers and trade publications, on college campuses, and by referrals from other sources.

The hospital offers its employees a number of training and career development programs. It also promotes continuing education through tuition assistance, reimbursement benefits, and work-study programs. The atmosphere is a highly supportive one that supports and encourages career development.

What to Expect

Changes in the health care industry and in insurance practices in recent years have forced many hospitals to reexamine how they do business and to focus more on the bottom line. Beth Israel Corporation is no exception, and its merger with Pathway Health Network is just one indication of the trend towards economizing and combining resources with other health care providers to produce a more cost-efficient manner of approaching patient care. Large hospitals such as BIH must now compete with health maintenance organizations to attract patients and comply with ever-changing insurance standards. This frequently results in staff and benefit reductions and merging of common functions to form a more economical operating system. Beth Israel Deaconess Medical Center, like many other hospital organizations, must work to retain a foothold in the rapidly changing world of health care.

Potent Quote

"Last year, over 40,000 patients were evaluated and treated in the [Beth Israel Deaconess] Emergency unit.... In this period in which managed care wields a growing influence on prehospital care, the [Emergency Medical Services] unit has been very active in the development of policies and procedures for the safe and efficient transfer of patients from one health care facility to another."

(From the organization's web site.)

Big Brothers Big Sisters of America

> *230 North 13th Street*
> *Philadelphia PA 19107*
> *215/567-7000*
> *World Wide Web: http://www.bbbsa.org/*
> *Contact: Arlene Boyd*

Overview

Founded in 1904, the group is the oldest mentoring organization serving youth in the United States.

By the Numbers

Big Brothers Big Sisters of America (BBSA) now serves over 100,000 children and youth in over 500 agencies across America. Much of the organization's funding comes through public and private gifts.

The Mission

The organization describes its goal as developing "the resources, environment and mechanisms to provide caring adults in the life of every child in need."

Words to the Wise

Questions concerning employment openings may be forwarded to the Philadelphia office.

What to Expect

As the organization approaches its hundredth anniversary, it is working to fulfill its commitment to the landmark Presidents' Summit by doubling the number of children it serves nationwide—and simultaneously providing community service opportunities for participants—by the end of the year 2000. The group has vowed to continue to grow while "maintaining our high standards of excellence for America's youth."

Potent Quote

"Big Brothers Big Sisters of America is the acknowledged leader in building professionally supported, dynamic relationships which unite children with committed volunteers, primarily on a one-to-one basis, transforming their lives, and enriching families, communities, and society. Our work is as elementary as putting a friend in a child's life, and as essential as putting hope into a child's future. To achieve our vision we will continue to build on our century-long history of commitment to excellence and of valuing all individuals, respecting their efforts, abilities, and differences."

(From the organization's web site.)

Boys and Girls Clubs of America

1230 West Peachtree Street, NW, Atlanta, Georgia 30309
404/815-5700
World Wide Web: http://www.bgca.org/
Contact: Linda Utterback

Overview

Geared toward promoting and assisting the nation's young people, the Boys and Girls Clubs of America (BGCA) provides programs in leadership training and development at some 1,850 facilities throughout the country. It supports the formation of community youth projects, provides on-site assistance to member clubs, and establishes new clubs in communities where no clubs are currently present. BGCA is a large organization, with affiliated clubs in all fifty states, Puerto Rico, and the Virgin Islands, all working to instill values and confidence in the leaders of tomorrow. From education to the environment, from the arts to business, from gang prevention to leadership development, BGCA is the premier program in the country for teaching young people the life skills they need to survive and succeed.

By the Numbers

Staff: 151 (Atlanta);
7,000 trained professional youth workers;
19,200 part-time staff members.

Budget: $432,000,000 (for all Clubs and national organization).

BGCA has been America's fastest-growing youth development organization, having experienced a 102-percent increase in youth served annually and a 68-percent increase in the number of their Clubs since 1987. Gifts from foundations, corporations, individuals, grants, and trust funds make up 70 percent of BGCA's income; the remaining 30 percent comes from dues and investments. The organization is able to spend 80 percent of its income on programs and services. The remainder is used for administrative expenses, including just 5 percent for fundraising. Each local Club is a private, not-for-profit agency whose policies are set by a volunteer board consisting of local residents. BGCA has been ranked among the top ten nonprofit organizations in the country by *The Chronicle of Philanthropy*, which also ranked it Number 1 among youth organizations.

The Mission

The Boys and Girls Club of America works to assist and support youth of all backgrounds in becoming responsible citizens and future leaders. It is the only national youth agency whose mission places a special emphasis on helping young people who are struggling to rise above disadvantaged conditions. With the assistance of corporate partnerships and others, BGCA works to find innovative ways for the youth of America to realize their full potential.

Words to the Wise

The organization's greatest need is for full-time, trained youth development professionals. At the Atlanta headquarters and throughout many of the local Clubs, basic administrative staff support is needed in a variety of areas. Ultimately, volunteerism is the primary power source for the movement, and may provide the best avenue into the organization.

What to Expect

BGCA makes a strong and positive impact on young lives through programs that build self-esteem and the development of values and skills necessary to personal growth in children. Over 2,600,000 girls and boys are served annually. Currently BGCA services 787 local Club organizations, and supports club facilities in diverse locations, including 289 Clubs in public housing. Over 71 percent of its constituency live in urban or inner-city areas, which in itself makes a powerful statement on the organization's behalf.

Working for BGCA would provide a rich sense of satisfaction for someone committed to making a difference in the lives of young people and supporting the development of the country's future leaders.

Potent Quote

"People Make the Difference: One of the factors which distinguish Boys & Girls Clubs is our professional staff. Every Club has full-time, trained youth development professionals, providing children with positive role models and mentors. In addition, thousands of volunteers provide vital supplementary support from within the community."

(From the organization's web site.)

Boy Scouts of America

> *1325 West Walnut Hill Lane, PO Box 152079, Irving, Texas 75015-2079*
> *972/580-2000*
> *World Wide Web: http://www.bsa.scouting.org*
> *Contact: National office or local BSA council service center*

Overview

The parent organization for all Boy Scout chapters, the Boy Scouts of America (BSA), provides assistance and support to local councils through its administration of standards in such areas as planning, training, conferences, finances, and membership rights. In addition, the organization provides materials and literature, insurance, and other services to local councils, and develops basic programs. Founded in 1910 and chartered by Congress in 1916, the BSA has four membership divisions. In addition to Boy Scouting, these include Cub Scouting, Exploring, and Learning for Life. It is one of the country's leaders in building effective character, good citizenship, a solid education, and personal fitness training for the country's youth.

By the Numbers

Staff: 1,040 paid staff; 1,200,000 volunteers.

Currently the BSA boasts over 5.3 million members. The National Council is supported by annual member registration fees, charter and service fees paid by the local councils, special gifts and bequests, and fund-raising campaigns, as well as income from the sales of magazines and Scouting equipment. Programs and services, including field operations, program development, and insurance/benefit costs, account for 63 percent of the BSA's $73 million in expenditures. An additional 15 percent is put into administration and fund-raising. The remainder represents increases in net assets through investments. Local councils, which are chartered by the parent organization, are funded largely by community endowments from the United Way and others, which the BSA works to strengthen through special fund-raising events. Income is also raised through foundation grants, investments, and special contributions. Youth members pay dues to their own pack or troop and can earn additional monies for their units through approved fund-raising projects. These local and national mechanisms have provided financial stability for the BSA at all levels.

The Mission

Boy Scouts of America seeks to help young people achieve their full potential by instilling values and preparing them for the moral and ethical choices they will have to face in their lives, thereby providing a service not only to the country's youth but to all citizens. The values the BSA seeks to instill are contained within the Scout Oath and Law. BSA strives to build character and develop the leaders of tomorrow.

Words to the Wise

The BSA is largely a volunteer-driven organization, but professionals are hired at both the local and national level to work with these volunteers and with community leaders in order to recruit, train, and guide them in Scouting programs. Hiring fields include a network of Customer Service staff trained to assist local units and their communities, ensuring that their needs are met and necessary materials for their program development are provided. Sales staff oversee the extension of Scouting to other community-based organizations, while those working in Finance are responsible for securing proper financial support for local councils. Public Relations professionals develop good working relationships between the councils and their communities and also publicize Scouting's story and goals. These are the primary areas in which one might become a professional Scouter. Another point of entry may be to become a volunteer in any one of the approximately 342 local councils.

What to Expect

Membership in all BSA programs is on the rise. Boy scouting now serves more than a million youths in the eleven-to-seventeen age range. The Exploring and Learning for Life programs are expanding and helping both boys and girls learn more about potential careers and develop positive skills, attitudes, and values. The BSA's strategic plan will put more of a focus on reaching and assisting urban families, strengthening unit relationships with the community, and improving public relations for the organization. As the need grows for the programs the BSA provides and the values it attempts to instill in the nation's youth, it is expected that membership will continue to rise.

Potent Quote

"The professional Scouter in an entry-level position is assigned to a district or service area within a local council. The job responsibilities are broad and varied. Duties include promoting, supervising, and working in the district or service area through volunteers. Different aspects of the professional Scouter's job include: Sales... Service... Finance... Administration... [and] Public Relations. If you are an adult and a college graduate, you may qualify to become a BSA professional. For more information call or visit the local council service center of the Boy Scouts of America, listed in the white pages of your telephone directory."

(From the organization's web site.)

Brigham & Women's Hospital, Inc.

75 Francis Street, Boston, Massachusetts 02115
617/732-5500
World Wide Web: http://www.partners.org/bwh/
Contact: Department of Human Resources/Employment

Overview
Brigham & Women's Hospital (BWH), which recently merged with Massachusetts General Hospital to form Partners Healthcare System, Inc., is one of the top-rated health care providers in the country. It has received international recognition for the quality of its facilities, service, and medical care.

By the Numbers

Staff: Approximately 8,000
(for parent company Brigham Medical Center, Inc.).

The organization's 702-bed facility offers "premier medical care and impeccable service and amenities befitting its dedication to quality." In 1993, BWH was selected as one of sixteen Vanguard Centers for participation in the Women's Health Initiative, the largest health research study of American women ever launched.

The Mission
Brigham & Women's Hospital is dedicated to serving the needs of the community and to providing the highest-quality health care to patients and their families. BWH is also committed to training the next generation of health care professionals and to extending the boundaries of medicine through basic and biomedical research. As part of Partners HealthCare System, the BWH intends to take a leadership role in developing an integrated health care network that will provide a full range of cost-effective, patient-centered services.

Words to the Wise

The BWH offers career opportunities in numerous areas, including: computer programming and analysis, human resources, medical technology, nursing management, and both physical and occupational therapy. Jobs are advertised through newspapers and trade journals as well as on college campuses. Management positions are generally selected from within the hospital, based on experience and demonstrated ability. BWH also offers summer internships and sponsors a work-study program.

The Department of Human Resources/Employment is cited as the first contact point for employment inquiries.

What to Expect

Although recognition and value are placed on the contributions of individuals, BWH emphasizes a spirit of teamwork among its employees. The primary goal, to which all are expected to make a contribution, is quality patient care and efficient delivery of service to the patient.

What to Expect

The emergence of HMOs and the growing influence of insurance companies in determining the course of patient care has brought changes to BWH in recent years. Though it maintains its reputation and tradition as a distinguished teaching hospital, it has also sought to grow with the times and adapt to modern needs and technologies. This was the basis for the 1994 formation of Partners HealthCare System, which allowed BWH to create an integrated health care delivery system with its affiliate, Massachusetts General Hospital. This initiative was carried further in 1996 with the establishment of Dana-Farber/Partners CancerCare, a joint training program in adult oncology involving the BWH, MGH, and Dana-Farber Cancer Institute. Meanwhile, BWH continues to set medical "firsts" in a number of areas and remains a firm fixture in annual lists of the best hospitals in the world.

Potent Quote

"*Vision.* To take a leadership role in creating a premier, patient-focused, integrated healthcare delivery system while enhancing our tradition as a distinguished academic medical institution. *Values.* Quality Patient Care: Delivering quality patient care is the center of everything we do. Teaching Excellence: We seek to uphold the highest standards in training health care professionals. Research Leadership: We continuously seek new ways to demonstrate our leadership role in research. Customer Focus: Our focus is to serve our customers. Respect for the Individual: We recognize and value the contributions of every individual. Teamwork: We work toward a unified approach to developing healthcare solutions. Embracing Change: Embracing change will help us to be successful. Operational Efficiency: We strive for efficient and effective delivery of services."

(From organization's vision and values statements.)

California Conservation Corps

1719 24th Street, Sacramento, California 95816-7114
916/341-3100
Recruitment Office: 916/341-3128 or (from inside California) 1-800-952-JOBS
E-mail recruitment information: recruit@ccc.ca.gov
World Wide Web: http://www.ccc.ca.gov/
Contact: Lynn Strickler

Overview

Through its mobilization of young people to aid and nurture the environment, the California Conservation Corps (CCC) has provided a twofold model—for youth employment and for the achievement of conservation goals throughout the world. Almost 60,000 young men and women have taken part in its programs, making the CCC the largest youth jobs corps in the U.S. It is also the oldest and largest conservation corps currently operating. Through CCC, three million hours a year are devoted to emergency assistance following natural disasters, stream restorations and projects to improve fish habitats, energy programs, a back-country trails program, and a wide range of other environmental projects. For its groundbreaking work in getting young people involved in state conservation efforts, the CCC has been awarded the United Nations Environmental Program Medal.

By the Numbers

Staff: 400.

Budget: $50,000,000.

The CCC is organized into northern and southern field divisions, with eleven districts and more than thirty satellite facilities located throughout the state. The CCC exists solely through government funding (such as the federal AmeriCorps program).

The Mission

The California Conservation Corps is a state agency with a dual mission: the protection of California's environment and resources and the employment and development of the state's youth. Men and women between the ages of eighteen and twenty-three are hired for one year and trained in a variety of tasks having to do with the management of natural resources. The basic, useful skills they acquire in the process assist them in future employment-seeking efforts.

Words to the Wise

The CCC employs 75 administrative staff and 325 field staff, with some part-time employees and volunteers. Jobs are advertised through newspapers and job fairs, as well as by word of mouth. The CCC provides opportunities in both urban and rural areas, some residential, some not. There is also an Australian work exchange. However, the primary call is for California residents between nineteen and twenty years old. Those who become corps members will work harder than they have ever worked in their lives, and for minimal wages, for one entire year. In the process, they will gain training and expertise in a variety of environmental programs and have experiences and educational opportunities that will benefit them for a lifetime. Corps members sometimes go on to further employment with the CCC.

Despite its daunting motto ("Hard work, low pay, miserable conditions, and more!") over 65,000 young men and women have participated in the CCC since it was established in 1976. The organization provides an excellent means for instilling values and ethics in its youthful employees, including a spirit of teamwork, an attendance to punctuality and self-discipline, and a willingness to work hard. Corps members take justifiable pride in their accomplishments and go on to find employment in all segments of the workplace. All are required to take tuition-reimbursed classes, whether studying for a GED or for a college-level degree, and all take classes in career planning and environmental awareness. The benefits to members are significant, and most appear to feel that their hard work is worthwhile.

What to Expect

Whether one serves as a corps member or an employee, the CCC offers a twofold sense of fulfillment: that of helping others discover the satisfaction of self-discipline and hard work, and that of helping the environment. This is a great place to work if environmental preservation and the development of the nation's youth are among your favorite concerns. If you're thinking of signing on as a corps members, just be aware that the routine can be an exhausting one.

Potent Quote

"The CCC follows in the footsteps of the federal Civilian Conservation Corps of the 1930s.... The CCC has been the model for youth corps programs on the local, state, and national levels and [has] attracted inquiries and visitors from more than 45 foreign countries. Along with its day-to-day conservation work, the CCC has become known as one of California's premier emergency response forces. When floods, fires, oil spills or earthquakes occur, the Corps can provide assistance within hours."

(From the organization's web site.)

Cedars-Sinai Medical Center (CSMC)

> *8723 Alden Drive, ASB1, Los Angeles, California 90048*
> *310/855-5521 (Job line)*
> *World Wide Web: http://www.csmc.edu/*
> *Contact: Human Resources*

Overview

Cedars-Sinai Medical Center, an internationally renowned, university-affiliated teaching and research program, is also the largest nonprofit hospital in the western United States. Its state-of-the-art facilities are located on the west side of Los Angeles. Cedars-Sinai's humanistic approach to patients is inspired by the ethical and cultural precepts of the Judaic tradition. It is among the nation's leaders in clinical care and bio-medical research and attracts some of the best physicians, scientists, and other health professionals in the world.

By the Numbers

Staff: Over 1,900 physicians; many more employees in other areas.

Over 200 residents and fellows are also employed. Cedars-Sinai offers over a thousand patient beds and "more than 100" forms of service to its community. The organization describes itself as "the largest nonprofit hospital in the western United States."

The Mission

Cedars-Sinai Medical Center has a threefold mission: delivery of top-quality health care services to patients and to the community at large; biomedical research to expand medical knowledge; and education of physicians and other health care professionals for the purpose of pro-viding better clinical care. CSMC is solicitous of each patient's dignity and needs, and works to provide the most advanced and sensitive care it can. It also provides health education to the community to facilitate early diagnosis and prevention of disease.

Words to the Wise

Job recruitment focuses on nursing and allied health professions. Cedars-Sinai seeks nurses, physical therapists, medical and radiological technologists, and nuclear medicine technicians. There are also openings for support staff, especially secretaries. Jobs are advertised primarily in local newspapers and trade journals.

Preference for hiring and promotion is generally given to persons of demonstrated ability already employed by Cedars-Sinai. Employees are evaluated regularly, and encouragement and support are provided to keep personnel fully current in their specialties.

What to Expect

Keeping pace with the changes in the health care field in recent years, Cedars-Sinai has become a fully integrated health care delivery system, with a network of primary-care physicians providing the best patient-oriented services to the community. It has earned a reputation as one of the finest health care facilities in the nation, while remaining in the vanguard of modern biomedical research. With its history of scientific success and high-quality patient care, it is expected to remain among the nation's leaders in health care, in community education and services, and in the identification of newer, more effective approaches to the prevention and treatment of disease.

Potent Quote

"Fundamental to maintaining the highest standards of patient care is our historic commitment to 'bench to bedside' research, assuring that our patients are among the first to benefit from scientific discovery. Over the last fifty years, our distinguished physician researchers have made contributions advancing many medical fields, including cardiology, genetics, organ transplantation, kidney disease, and neonatal intensive care. These men and women are internationally recognized for their innovative research and their medical breakthroughs. For example, in use worldwide are two pioneering devices developed at Cedars-Sinai; the Swan-Ganz Catheter to monitor blood flow of cardiac patients and the excimer laser used in a wide range of procedures from clearing blocked arteries to correcting nearsightedness."

Center for Science in the Public Interest

1875 Connecticut Avenue NW, Suite 300, Washington DC 20009
202/332-9110
202/332-9110 ext. 116 (job line)
Fax: 202/265-4954
World Wide Web: http://www.cspinet.org/
Contact: Human Resources Department

Overview

Founded in 1971 by three scientists and an attorney interested in public advocacy and science, the organization is a nonprofit advocacy and education group dedicated to improving the safety and nutritional quality of the food supply, and to reducing the damage associated with alcohol.

By the Numbers

The Center for Science in the Public Interest (CSPI) oversees a budget of over $13 million. It is supported by over 1,000,000 member-subscribers to its publication *Nutrition Action Healthletter* and by means of sales of educational materials and grants from foundations.

The Mission

CSPI works to "promote health through educating the public about nutrition and alcohol," and seeks to ensure that advances in science are used for the public's good. Over the years, it has mounted a number of highly visible media campaigns meant to draw the public's attention to various nutrition- and alcohol-related issues.

Words to the Wise

As of this writing, the organization's web site features information on current employment openings. A variety of internships are available.

What to Expect

The organization has a history of growth and avid interest and support from its members, and appears well positioned to continue to pursue its mission.

Potent Quote

"CSPI is an aggressive nonprofit consumer organization conducting innovative programs in nutrition, alcohol, and food safety."

(From the organization's web site.)

Chesapeake Bay Foundation

162 Prince George Street, Annapolis, Maryland 21401
301/627-4393
Contact: Michael Heller

Overview

Though technically limited to a narrow geographic area, the goals and methods of the Chesapeake Bay Foundation (CBF) can serve as a model for innovative environmental preservation programs around the country. Many of the projects and issues CBF has tackled through its Claggett Farm Education Center, for instance, have been developed to demonstrate that conservation pursuits need not alienate members of the business community or threaten corporate profits.

The foundation targets numerous areas for legislative advocacy and public education, including oil drilling, use of pesticides, improvement of water quality, regulation of land use, and disposal of toxic wastes. Key to the foundation's mission has been the 1972 Clean Water Act, which regulates pollution in all water areas, and which the foundation seeks to protect from weakening by acts of Congress.

By the Numbers

Staff: 118.

Budget: $6,730,000.

Funding for the CBF is achieved through a combination of gifts and grants (43 percent), membership contributions (35 percent), tuition and education contracts (13 percent), and income from investments and the sales of merchandise (8 percent). Most of this funding goes toward programs, projects, and public education. Some is reserved for lobbying, litigation, and publication costs.

The Mission

The Chesapeake Bay Foundation is devoted to the conservation and restoration of the Chesapeake Bay. Its targets are the preservation of the Clean Water Act, the safe and effective management of land-use, and countering urban sprawl with a program of urban revitalization. The foundation also seeks to find ways to work with the business community, particularly the building industry, to ensure that it does not suffer economic penalties when it takes steps to protect the environment.

Words to the Wise

CBF employees are committed to environmental work. Field educators and issue experts make up the largest part of its staff . In addition to office support staff, there is a need for fund raisers and writers/editors. Part-time and summer employees are limited to about two interns a year. The CBF also relies heavily on its corps of about 250 volunteers, which may provide another point of entry. Jobs are advertised via newspapers and environmental publications.

What to Expect

With 83,000 highly motivated members and an increase in donations in recent years as a result of public concern over environmental issues, the CBF is likely to continue to be an active participant in the environmental nonprofit arena for many years to come. In particular, its voice is likely to be heard, and its membership appealed to for support, as long as there are legislative and judicial battles over the Clean Water Act.

The CBF offers one of the most effective and creative long-term strategies for protecting the environment while also protecting the legitimate rights of industry. It is ideal for those who have a special interest in these areas. Although benefits are offered, many jobs at the CBF do not pay at the level of the for-profit sector. For those who are willing to accept these financial limitations, however, CBF offers significant emotional rewards.

Potent Quote

"Typically, a tension has built up which maintains that the process of protecting the environment has hindered the business community.... We need to find ways to work together toward common goals."

(Thomas V. Grasso, executive director,
quoted in the *Baltimore Business Journal*.)

Chicanos Por La Causa, Inc. (CPLC)

> *1112 East Buckeye Road, Phoenix, Arizona 85034-4043*
> *602/257-0700*
> *Fax: 602/246-2740*
> *World Wide Web: http://www.azstarnet.com/~cplc/*
> *Contact: Liz Loyola*

Overview

Begun as an advocacy group in 1969, Chicanos por la Causa has since developed into one of the largest Community Development Corporations (CDCs) in the nation, providing services and assistance in economic development to help improve the quality of life for its constituents. Along with social services, CPLC provides a variety of cultural and economic programs within the community, including small business loans, development of youth leadership and education, housing opportunities and funding, and job training/employment assistance. With client bases in several Arizona regions, the organization also leads numerous residential, commercial, and industrial development projects designed for the welfare of Arizonans from all sides of the social and economic spectrum. However, advocacy for the socially and economically disadvantaged remains its primary cause; its goal is to assist all individuals within the community to achieve self-sufficiency.

By the Numbers

Staff: 350.

Budget: Approximately $7,000,000 (latest figure available).

Since the mid-1970s, when it began to expand its goals and services, the CPLC has become one of the premier Latino community development corporations in the country. It has attracted significant public and private support, with 95 percent of its funding coming from grants and the remainder derived from foundations and individual contributions. The organization suffered some setbacks during the early 1980s as a result of federal cutbacks, which forced it to abandon one of its key programs. A major reduction in staff and operating budget followed. However, with the help of social service contracts with state and city agencies, and support for its core administrative operations provided by a number of foundations, it slowly recovered. Since then it has maintained a diverse base of funding and a profit-generating plan bolstered by economic development ventures.

The Mission

CPLC is a Community Development Organization whose overall goal of helping its client base achieve greater opportunity, dignity, and self-sufficiency through cultural and economic programs and social services—all designed to counteract the effects of poverty within the community. To this end CPLC works to assist people in obtaining stable, meaningful employment, affordable, high-quality housing, and access to useful educational opportunities. The organization provides counseling services, budgeting and intervention advocacy, home and small business loans, emergency utility assistance, youth development activities, and more; it also manages an apartment complex for elderly and disabled residents. CPLC leadership believes that the poor and needy can overcome obstacles if they are provided with the opportunity to explore and develop their potential for self-sufficiency and independence from welfare programs. It advocates improved access to educational and other opportunities as a primary strategy supporting this goal.

Early leader Joe Eddie Lopez recalled the group's founding in this way: "We were primarily interested in raising the consciousness of the remainder of society to the problems that Mexican Americans were facing throughout the state. We were interested in meeting and confronting the education establishment, and meeting and confronting the government officials, because we didn't think that they were employing enough of our people." (Pratt Institute Center for Community and Environmental Development oral history project.)

Words to the Wise

Since today's CPLC is an organization primarily devoted to social services, the greatest need is for counselors and caseworkers. A background in social work is probably the greatest asset for employment. There are usually about ten staff openings per year, most of them for counselors, although the need occasionally arises for office managers, bookkeepers, and fund-raisers in the main Phoenix office and in satellite offices in Somerton, Nogakes, and Tucson. As with many similar organizations, volunteerism may be one way to get your foot in the door, as CPLC counts on the support of over 5,000 volunteers. Job openings are usually advertised internally, but they may also be posted at local colleges or advertised in local papers.

What to Expect

The CPLC is in good shape these days. Having overcome the financial hardships of the 1980s, it has succeeded in expanding the scope of its vision and the opportunities it offers to the community. Its wide range of services is available to diverse segments of the Latino population of Arizona, including the poor and homeless, the elderly, immigrants and migrant workers, the handicapped, substance abusers, and teenage parents. It has enjoyed tremendous growth and success in recent years and has had an important impact on the Mexican-American community. The organization is likely to continue to play a key role in Arizona's economic and cultural development for some time to come.

CPLC has become a large, prestigious and comparatively stable organization, offering ample opportunities for those who want to work in community service. As with many organizations in the nonprofit sector, however, the starting pay is very low, and may not improve over time. Dedication to CPLC's cause must be your prime motivating factor in seeking employment.

Potent Quote

"Chicanos Por La Causa, Inc. (CPLC) is a community development corporation... formed in 1969 by a group of young men and women of Mexican descent who were concerned with the growing problems that plagued members of the poor, largely Hispanic South Phoenix community, many of whom were transitory, of low educational attainment, and unemployed.... CPLC's social service programs [now] offer food assistance, advocacy, counseling, and information and referral services. CPLC has joined with a number of local agencies to develop and maintain community-based educational services....[and] offers technical assistance to help minority businesses establish a firm foundation."

(Office of Minority Health Resource Center report.)

Children's Hospital Corporation/ Children's Hospital Medical Center

300 Longwood Avenue, Boston, Massachusetts 02115
617/355-6000
Fax: 617/730-0759
World Wide Web: http://www.childrenshospital.org/job
Contact: Human Resources Department

Overview

Children's Hospital Medical Center (CHMC) is the country's largest health care organization devoted to pediatrics. It is also home to the world's largest pediatric research facility, the John J. Enders Pediatric Research Laboratories. Founded in 1869, CHMC is the primary pediatric teaching hospital of the Harvard Medical School and operates a number of other health care facilities in the Greater Boston area, as well as a variety of contracted clinical services. It offers a complete range of health care services for patients from birth through age twenty-one (and sometimes older). CHMC maintains a reputation for quality, excellence, and prestige that places it at the top of the list of best pediatric hospitals in the United States.

By the Numbers

Staff: 3,200.

Annual Revenues: $340,800,000.

The organization boasts 300 beds and a professional staff of over 1,100. It is responsible for management of the Children's Extended Care Center in Groton, Massachusetts, and was ranked as the #1 hospital specializing in pediatric care in America for eight consecutive years by *USA TODAY.*

The Mission

Children's Hospital Medical Center is dedicated to high-quality patient care, scientific research, and medical training. It seeks to enhance the health and well-being of children and families in the community; to be a leader in research and discovery, seeking new approaches to the prevention, diagnosis, and treatment of childhood diseases; and to educate future leaders in pediatric health care.

Words to the Wise

Qualified candidates with degrees in nursing and the life sciences may well find rich opportunities for employment at CHMC and its affiliated clinics and health care facilities. In addition to openings in medicine and surgery, there are specialty sub-units such as cardiac care, neurology, psychiatric treatment, and intensive care. There is also a great need for administrative support from secretaries, clerks, accountants, administrative assistants, etc. Those with strong office skills will find numerous openings in a variety of units and offices. Management opportunities exist for those with a master's degree or higher. Summer internships are also available, and there is a core volunteer staff that provides invaluable support in many areas.

The hospital's management encourages the nurturing and development of careers. Development programs are offered to assist nurses in keeping their licensure current, tuition assistance is made available for career-related studies, and numerous educational workshops and interdisciplinary conferences are offered within and without the hospital. CHMC is a truly supportive, caring environment that encourages personal and professional achievement in its employees while emphasizing such values as quality, equality, diversity, and compassion.

What to Expect

The Center is large and offers numerous opportunities for growth and advancement in a variety of areas, both professional and non-professional. Participation in its mission to provide the best in pediatric care can result in a deep sense of personal satisfaction for those who love and want to help children.

Potent Quote

"As a major pediatric referral center, Children's Hospital's mission is to provide the highest-quality health care. It is also the hospital's mission to enhance the health and well-being of the children and families in our local community. In support of this mission, Children's strives to be the leading source for research and discovery, seeking new approaches to the prevention, diagnosis, and treatment of childhood diseases, as well as to educate the next generation of leaders in child health."

(From the organizations' mission statement.)

The Children's Museum of Boston

300 Congress Street, Boston, Massachusetts 02210
617/426-6500
Fax: 617/426-1944
Contact: Human Resources

Overview

The Children's Museum of Boston works to provide interactive exhibits and special activities for children of all social and cultural backgrounds. It has earned a national reputation for the currency and quality of its programs and presentations.

By the Numbers

Staff: 210.

Attracting over 400,000 visitors annually, the Children's Museum of Boston is the second-largest children's museum in the country and the third-oldest worldwide. Its Cultural Collection contains over 30,000 objects reflecting daily life in cultures around the world.

The Mission

Established in 1913, the Children's Museum of Boston is an interactive museum devoted to the education and entertainment of children. It has been hailed as a pioneer in the field of interactive museum exhibitions. By focusing on current events, cross-cultural exploration, and compelling, immediately accessible science exhibits, the Children's Museum aims to open up new horizons for the children who visit its facility.

Words to the Wise

Full and part-time jobs are available in several areas, but the focus is primarily on museum guides/exhibit interpreters. For many applicants, the best way to become a member of the Museum staff may be through its internship program, which offers a small stipend for five weeks during the school year and three months during the summer, as well as occasional internships of ten months' duration. While students are preferred, non-students (career changers and individuals re-entering the work force) are occasionally accepted. An interest in teaching, science, or the arts is preferred. Job candidates from outside the U.S. are also considered for the internship program.

What to Expect

Expect a high-energy work environment and an organizational commitment to the development of dramatic, innovative, high-impact museum exhibits for children.

If you don't like kids or—let's be honest—if you don't have a high tolerance for noise, you may want to think twice before applying for an internship or a staff position here.

Potent Quote

"[An] interactive museum dedicated to helping children understand and enjoy the world by concentrating on multiculturalism, small sciences, and social issues."

(Peterson's Internships, 1997.)

Children's National Medical Center

111 Michigan Avenue, NW, Washington, D.C. 10020-2916
202/745-5000
Fax: 202/884-5987
Contact: Sabrina Carter (for clerical and general employment)
World Wide Web: http://www.cnmc.org/

Overview
A pediatric hospital accommodating up to 279 patients, the Children's National Medical Center was founded in 1870 by Dr. Samuel Claggett Busey and other community leaders in the District of Columbia.

By the Numbers
Staff: 2,800.

The hospital accommodates up to 279 patients and is "ranked #6 in the United States among pediatric hospitals."

The Mission
Children's National Medical Center seeks to be the preeminent provider of quality pediatric health care in the D.C. area. In addition, CNMC works to improve the health and well-being of children by pursuing excellence in patient care, scientific research, education, and advocacy efforts.

Words to the Wise
CNMC has recently expanded its facilities in numerous areas, including information systems, billing and receivables systems, and computer networking. It has also upgraded its off-site practice facilities. There is a strong need for skilled network engineers, database managers, systems

analysts, and technical support people, and others wishing to pursue opportunities in health care information technology.

Licensed nurses are also needed. The organization's web site advertises "outstanding career opportunities for nurses to join our team of highly skilled professionals. Our environment is fast-paced and challenging."

Job opportunities in numerous other disciplines are advertised through newspapers, trade journals, and employment and state job agencies. Qualified personnel are also recruited at job fairs and trade shows. Paid internships are available.

What to Expect

CNMC supports career development and provides special training programs, classes and workshops. Employees are encouraged to participate in job and trade fairs and in professional associations. Tuition assistance and reimbursement are also offered to those seeking further educational opportunities. CNMC generally promotes from within, so that once you are established, you may have ample opportunity for advancement.

Potent Quote

"Our mission is to be the preeminent provider of quality health care services to infants, children, and youth in our region. Children's National Medical Center will strive to enhance the health and well-being of children through responsible programs for excellence in care, advocacy, research, and education."

(From the organization's web site.)

Clean Water Action

> *1320 18th Street, NW, Suite 300, Washington, D.C. 20036*
> *202/895-0420*
> *World Wide Web: http://essential.org/cwa/office.htm*
> *Contact: Casey Calloway*

Overview

Based in Washington, and with offices in other parts of the country, Clean Water Action is a national citizen's organization whose work has covered such areas as the management of toxic waste, safety issues in the workplace and the community at large, recycling, alternative energy technologies, protection of the Florida Everglades, and reauthorization of the Clean Water Act. The organization strives to achieve its goals through a combination of public education, organization on the community level, research, lobbying, publications, and training and technical assistance.

By the Numbers

Staff: 445 full-time; 100 part-time; 150 summer employees.

Budget: $11,000,000.

The majority of all Clean Water Action funding comes from contributions obtained via telephone and canvassing. Other sources are foundations, giving campaigns in local businesses, and government grants at the federal, state, and local levels.

The Mission

Clean Water Action works to ensure water for citizens that is clean, safe, and affordable. Its other environmental concerns include the protection of natural resources and the control of toxic materials. The organization also works on strategies to create conservation-oriented jobs.

Words to the Wise

The largest segment of Clean Water Action's work force is devoted to canvassing for funds, with the remainder providing organizational and office support. Jobs are advertised through environmental, social, and economic justice groups, through national and local publications, and through colleges and universities. Up to ten interns a year are also accepted in both paid and unpaid positions.

What to Expect

Expect long hours, comparatively low (starting) pay, and the satisfaction of working with people who are deeply committed to improve water quality nationwide. There are opportunities here, but they are not likely to be satisfying for those who do not believe passionately in the cause on which Clean Water Action is founded. If you do not have deep feelings about improving water quality, this is not the organization for you.

Potent Quote

"[Clean Water Action works for] clean, safe and affordable water, [and the] prevention of health-threatening pollution."

(From the organization's web site.)

Cleveland Clinic Foundation

9500 Euclid Avenue, Cleveland, Ohio 44195-0001
216/444-2705 (Job line)
World Wide Web: http://www.ccf.org/
Contact: Human Resources

Overview

The Cleveland Clinic Foundation, founded in 1921, is one of the world's first and largest group practices, with over 850 physicians in more than 100 specialties and subspecialties. The Clinic provides a 1,000-bed teaching hospital, an outpatient clinic, and a facility for research in basic and medical science. It was founded on the principle that patients receive the best possible care when clinical practice is conducted in collaboration with research and education. It has taken a unique approach to the group practice philosophy, requiring that its primary decision-makers and Board of Governors be practicing physicians. The Cleveland Clinic has consistently been rated as one of the ten best hospitals in the United States. In 1997, it combined with several other hospitals and health care systems to form the Cleveland Clinic Health System, providing improved patient care quality and lower costs to a broad area of Northeast Ohio residents.

By the Numbers

Staff: 8,200.

In a recent year, Cleveland Clinic physicians oversaw 1,182,3000 outpatient visits and 49,987 hospital admissions. According to the organization's press materials: "For each of the past six years, the magazine *U.S. News and World Report* has recognized the quality of medical care at the Cleveland Clinic by distinguishing it as one of the ten best hospitals in the United States."

The Cleveland Clinic Foundation relies heavily for its funding on philanthropic donations and community support. Grants fund much of its research. The Clinic recently launched a five-year capital campaign entitled "Securing the 21st Century," with the goal of developing new clinical treatments, expanding its research efforts, maintaining important programs, and increasing its endowment. With its reputation for high-quality medical care and research, the Foundation has long been one of the best-supported, most prosperous hospitals in the country.

The Mission

The Cleveland Clinic Foundation's motto is "better care of the sick, investigation into their problems, and the further education of all those who serve the sick." The Clinic combines clinical and hospital care with research and education in a private, nonprofit group practice.

Words to the Wise

Medical technologists and nurses are frequently sought, in addition to basic administrative and office support staff. There are also work-study programs for students.

What to Expect

With its strong base of support and excellent reputation, the Cleveland Clinic Foundation's future appears to be very secure. Its current efforts to develop new treatments and technologies for improved patient care will only enhance its image.

Potent Quote

"Certainly, the Cleveland Clinic has prospered over the years because of its excellence in medical care and research. However, it has taken more than that to keep this nonprofit institution on top. The commitment by people in the community to support us with their time and money has left a significant mark on what the Cleveland Clinic is today."

(Floyd D. Loop, M.D., CEO of the Cleveland Clinic Foundation.)

Close Up Foundation

> *44 Canal Center Plaza, Alexandria, Virginia 22314*
> *703/706-3300*
> *World Wide Web: http://www.closeup.org/*
> **Contact: Mary Rogers, Human Resource Director**

Overview

Born of the idea that the best chance for young people to change the current political system is by learning to work within it—and that Washington, D.C. provided "the greatest classroom in the world"—the Close Up Foundation was established in 1970 to provide a way to bring students closer to the government by way of sound civic education. Teachers are trained intensively in strategies that can be applied in the classroom and in the field. Close Up's programs provide important insights into current events and a way to involve students in civic affairs nationwide.

By the Numbers

Staff: 180-250.

Budget: $34,000,000.

Tuition fees make up 70 percent of Close Up's funding, with an additional 14 percent provided by the government and 8 percent by foundations.

The Mission

Close Up Foundation provides citizenship education programs to teach students of all ages and backgrounds about their rights and responsibilities as citizens. Students learn how to be active and effective participants in the democratic process, both within and beyond their own community. Teachers learn the skills needed to transmit and build upon that knowledge. Civic involvement becomes a lifelong commitment.

As the foundation puts it: "Civic learning is for everyone. Civic involvement is a lifelong process. We learn best through direct experience."

Words to the Wise

At this time the greatest need within the organization appears to be for Program Instructors. This position does not require teacher certification or experience, only an interest in government and civic affairs and a willingness to teach high school and middle school students. Close Up will provide the training. Over ninety Program Instructors are employed each year to take part in a nontraditional educational setting. Educators are supported by a staff of organizers, writers, typists, and bookkeepers; there are also occasional openings for fund raisers, researchers, and office support staff. There are typically at least fifty staff openings a year, advertised through college placement offices and in regional and Washington, D.C. newspapers. Hours are long, and pay scales may be a problem for some applicants, although benefits are offered.

Close Up works closely with schoolteachers to strengthen existing programs in civic education. Its successful Washington High School Program for Teachers, its summer institutes, and its international exchanges are all aimed at expanding teachers' roles. Such initiatives focus on educating the teacher in methods and techniques that can then be brought back to the classroom. The Close Up courses are short and intense and stress active learning, on-site studies, critical thinking, and diversity, as well as important community concepts. It is a rich educational culture for all who become involved with the organization.

What to Expect

Close Up was originally founded to help students learn about American-style democracy and to train better citizens. Today there is a keen awareness that cynicism toward government and politics has fostered an attitude of apathy and helplessness among young people—in sharp contrast to the social activism of the 1960s and 1970s. Close Up sees its mission as more crucial than ever, in a world that is changing rapidly, both technologically and socially, and in which more and more countries struggle toward democratic systems of governing. It plans to step up its efforts to promote good citizenship and the values of a strong civic education, in order to create a stable social and democratic environment for future generations. Greater emphasis will likely be placed on the needs of teachers, and initiatives will continue to be developed to provide a variety of educational opportunities and in-service training.

Close Up's nontraditional approach provides a unique setting in which to work. Its programs can be a rich learning experience for students and instructors alike. For those who want to make a difference in the values and civic involvement of the country's young people, working with Close Up can be a very rewarding experience.

Potent Quote

"The program draws on the vast political, cultural, and historical resources of Washington—from the U.S. Capitol to the Smithsonian's Museum of American History to the Vietnam Veterans Memorial. Visits to these sites, however, avoid the typical tourist approach by looking beyond the marble and granite. Each site, with its symbolic connection to the American experience, is used as a springboard to substantive discussions over issues on the national agenda."

(*Social Studies* magazine, September/October, 1993.)

Colonial Williamsburg Foundation, Inc.

PO Box 1776, Williamsburg, Virginia 23187-1776
757/220-7001
Contact: Recruiting Specialist
24-hour Job Line: 757-220-7129
World Wide Web: http://www.history.org/
Contact: Human Resources

Overview

Best known for its historic restoration of Williamsburg, Virginia (begun in 1926 by John D. Rockefeller, Jr.), the Colonial Williamsburg Foundation also owns and operates eleven restaurants and four hotels, by which it provides numerous employment opportunities. The cornerstone of the Foundation is the preservation and restoration of eighteenth-century Williamsburg, the colonial capital of Virginia.

By the Numbers

Staff: 3,600.

Budget: $110,000,000.

With over 500 historic buildings covering 173 acres, Colonial Williamsburg is a tremendous historical and educational achievement, a living testament to the days when colonists were just beginning to form a remarkable nation.

The Mission

Colonial Williamsburg Foundation, Inc. is an educational organization devoted to the restoration, recreation, and interpretation of Williamsburg, Virginia. Now considered a national treasure, Colonial Williamsburg is a living history museum that aims to inspire and inform visitors about the historic capital, the events that occurred there, and the people of the eighteenth century who helped to shape the nation. High-quality hospitality and service are provided through the foundation's chain of restaurants and hotels.

Words to the Wise

At any given time the Foundation is likely to have a number of professional and technical positions open, in areas ranging from historical interpretation to historic site management, research and museum studies, archeology, and information management. There are also openings in culinary arts, hotel management, materials management, public relations, physical plant maintenance, and office and administrative support. Many positions require an advanced degree and knowledge in eighteenth-century history. Preference is usually given to internal job candidates, even when external candidates are equally qualified. Unpaid student and summer internships are also available to those seeking work experience in their selected field. Interns may work in any number of Foundation departments, including curating and tour presentations, costume design, development, communications, architectural research, and more. Job openings are posted throughout the foundation and are often filled through word-of-mouth. Specialized knowledge of eighteenth-century habits and skills (i.e., blacksmithing, weaving, etc.) can often pave the way to paid employment in Colonial Williamsburg. Experience in administration, sales, marketing, and hotels or restaurants can also be a plus.

The Colonial Williamsburg Foundation offers a supportive work environment and a clear set of organizational goals for all employees. To fulfill its commitment to ongoing education, it provides basic supervisory and management training through in-house courses as well as courses in specialized topics. Full tuition reimbursement is given for job-related seminars and classes, which are open and accommodating to people with disabilities. The Foundation seeks to keep the workplace drug- and alcohol-free, and to that end requires all final job candidates to go through a drug screening test and background investigation before hiring.

What to Expect

Colonial Williamsburg is one of the most popular tourist attractions in the country, with a highly successful education mission. Significant income from the Foundation's restaurants and hotels keeps the organization on a solid financial footing. These strengths make the Foundation a very secure place for employment.

Potent Quote

"Today, the Historic Area of Colonial Williamsburg is both a museum and a living city. Many of the restored and reconstructed homes and outbuildings are residences for Colonial Williamsburg's employees. And each year, nearly three million visitors join in the work of Mr. Rockefeller and Dr. [W.A.R.] Goodwin, [who each played such pivotal roles in launching the restoration effort]. Each purchase of Colonial Williamsburg Foundation tickets, lodging, meals, goods, or services is an investment in ongoing preservation, research, and education efforts. By supporting the nonprofit Foundation, each visitor helps to ensure that new generations may stand in wonder, touched by the lives, legends, and lessons of Williamsburg."

(From the organization's web site.)

Confederate Air Force

> *PO Box 62000, Midland, Texas 79711*
> *915/563-1000*
> *Fax: 915/563-8046*
> *Contact: Donna Blaylock, Human Resources*
> *World Wide Web: http://www.avdigest.com/caf/*

Overview

Founded in 1957, the Confederate Air Force (CAF) has accumulated a fleet of 136 aircraft that are flown in over 300 events each year to demonstrate the different types of airplanes used during World War II. The CAF sponsors war-related research programs and a speakers' bureau; it also maintains Second World War military aviation artifacts and memorabilia in its Combat Hall of Fame and Conventional Museum. With 89 regional groups, the organization has a membership base of 7,500. Members take part in annual air shows and exhibits and the semiannual Wing Staff Conference. They also publish numerous journals and newsletters devoted to aviation of 1939 to 1945.

By the Numbers

Staff: 30.

Budget: $2,000,000

Chartered as a non-profit charitable and educational corporation in Texas, the CAF relies heavily on endowments and donations. The American Airpower Heritage Foundation (AAHF) exists to seek funding for CAF programs. Earnings from the AAHF Endowment Fund are used to meet organizational goals and pay for key CAF programs.

The Mission

The Confederate Air Force is a multinational organization for individuals interested in the history and preservation of World War II military aircraft. Its twofold mission is to maintain World War II combat aircraft in flying condition and to provide an extensive museum devoted to the display and protection of these aircraft and to the memories of the people who built, maintained and flew them in our country's defense. The CAF strives to maintain an organization with a dedication, enthusiasm, and esprit de corps in keeping with the American military aviation heritage. Although the CAF's primary mission is the preservation of military aircraft and history, it considers its second-most-important mission to be the teaching of this history and especially the lessons learned about military preparedness and air power during World War II.

Words to the Wise

Questions concerning employment opportunities may be forwarded to the Midland office.

What to Expect

Although run by a small staff, the group comprises a huge, dedicated following of aviation enthusiasts who participate actively in its programs and goals. Interest and participation in the organization's activities appear likely to grow in coming years.

Potent Quote

"In 1957, four friends purchased a P-51 Mustang, each sharing in the $2,500 cost of the airplane… Legend has it that upon arriving at the Mercedes airfield in deep south Texas one Sunday morning in 1957, the group found that someone had painted a sign on the fuselage of the P-51 as a joke. The sign read '*Confederate Air Force.*' The pilots seemed pleased with the new name, saluted each other, and decided it should stay."

(From the organization's web site.)

Consumers Union

> *256 Washington Street, Mount Vernon, New York 10553*
> *914/378-2000*
> *Contact: Ms. England*

Overview

Publisher of *Consumer Reports*, along with other magazines, news-letters, and about thirty books each year, the Consumers Union was established in 1936. It has since become the best-known U.S. consumer resource for information and advice on commercial goods and services, health care, and finances. Based in Mount Vernon, New York, the Union also maintains offices in Washington, D.C., San Francisco, and Austin. It maintains three law offices whose staffs serve as advocates for the average U.S. consumer through the initiation of lawsuits, petitions to the government, commentary on upcoming government actions and legisla-tion, and testimony at legislative or regulatory hearings. The Consumers Union is thus a powerful advocate for the consumer.

By the Numbers

Staff: 348.

Budget: $76,000,000.

Publication sales account for 90 percent of Consumers Union's income. The remainder comes from individual contributions and from foundations.

The Mission

The primary goal of the Consumers Union is to provide consumers with the information and services they need to maintain and enhance their quality of life. Among its varied activities can be counted research, lobbying, community organizing, and public education; training and technical assistance; and a large number of publications.

Words to the Wise

The Consumers Union has about ten staff openings a year, chiefly for writers, editors, and attorneys. Support positions include researchers, managers, administrative assistants, and bookkeepers. There are a few positions available for part-time and summer employees, interns, and volunteers. Job openings are advertised in *Consumer Reports*, the *New York Times*, and various other newspapers.

What to Expect

The organization's activities are strongly focused on the rights and interests of American consumers. Those who do not possess a strong consumer-rights orientation, or whose values conflict with the basic legal, advocacy, and research aims of the organization, will not be good candidates for openings.

Potent Quote

"Consumers Union, publishers of *Consumer Reports*, is a non-profit, independent organization providing consumers with information on goods, services, health, and personal finance. We test and rate products and services. If a product is judged high in overall quality and relatively low in price, we deem it a "best buy".... Our Ratings and reports may not be used in advertising or for any other commercial purpose."

(From *Consumer Reports*.)

The Cousteau Society

870 Greenbrier Circle, Suite 402, Chesapeake, Virginia 23320
804/523-9335
1-800-441-4395
Fax: 804/523-1909
World Wide Web: http://www.cousteau.org/
Contact: Marcia Griffin

Overview

Founded in 1973 by the late Jacques Cousteau, the underwater explorer, the Cousteau Society has achieved fame through its numerous documentaries and educational programs, which are aimed at expanding public awareness of marine life and improving the planet's ecological future. The Society's best-known symbol is the *Calypso*, Cousteau's ship, which transported him and other researchers around the world in pursuit of a better understanding of earth's aquatic environment and the resources it provides.

By the Numbers

The Society—a U.S.-based nonprofit organization with a companion organization in Paris—is supported by over 150,000 dues-paying members. In addition to its Virginia office, the Cousteau Society operates two regional offices: one in Los Angeles and one in New York.

The Mission

The Cousteau Society works to improve the quality of life on the planet for all generations and to make the public aware of how our lives are linked to the oceans and marine life. It is a leader in the fight against water pollution and actively supports underwater exploration and an ecological investigation of the planet's water resources. Through such exploration, as well as through documentaries, educational programs, and many other activities, the Society works to inform the public about marine ecological issues, in the hope that intelligent decisions on the management of the world's natural resources will result.

Words to the Wise

Questions concerning employment openings may be forwarded to the Chesapeake office.

What to Expect

Prior to his death, Cousteau was working hard to establish the science called "ecotechnie," in the hope of making it part of university curricula everywhere. To that end, he became the first UNESCO-Cousteau Chair of Ecotechnie in Brussels in 1990. A discipline that combines a number of inter-related sciences, ecotechnie's goal is to provide universal management strategies that study and plan for the long-term effects of economic development on nature.

Cousteau's hope was to create "a new kind of decision-maker, educated to understand the connections between humanity and nature, who is concerned about the future and acknowledges value beyond simple economics." Despite its famous leader's passing, the Cousteau Society will continue to advance this vision, advocating a global approach to natural resource management and working toward building a world in which humankind will respect its environment. The Society has been lobbying for United Nations adoption of a "Bill of Rights for Future Generations" and managing numerous other projects.

Madame Jacques-Yves Cousteau now serves as President and CEO of the U.S. entity founded by her husband.

Potent Quote

"What we human beings are all living now… is an extraordinary, but exceptionally dangerous adventure. And we have a very small number of years left to fail or to succeed in providing a sustainable future to our species."

(Jaques-Yves Cousteau)

Dana-Farber Cancer Institute

> *44 Binney Street, Boston, Massachusetts 02115*
> *617/632-3052*
> *Fax: 617/632-4050*
> *Contact: Brenda Welch, Human Resources (general employment resumes);*
> *Peggy Koval, Human Resources (nursing resumes)*
> *World Wide Web: http://www.jimmyfund.com*

Overview

Established in 1947, Dana-Farber Cancer Institute (DFCI) is one of twenty-six cancer research and treatment centers designated as a comprehensive cancer center by the National Cancer Institute. It is a teaching affiliate of the Harvard Medical School and oversees research in five additional laboratories throughout Boston. In 1996, DFCI formed an agreement with Partners HealthCare System, Inc., to create a new program in adult medical oncology that would combine the research and medical resources of both institutions.

By the Numbers

Staff: 1,800.

DFCI's primary fund-raising source is the popular Jimmy Fund, which is supported by various prominent New England institutions, including the Boston Red Sox and the Massachusetts Chiefs of Police Association.

Words to the Wise

Questions concerning employment openings may be forwarded to the Boston office.

What to Expect

DFCI is one of the nation's premier cancer research and treatment institutes and will probably remain so. Its work has broadened somewhat in recent years; DFCI is now one of twelve federally designated centers for AIDS research.

The organization is vigorous and strongly positioned to pursue its organizational goals. It is among the most stable and respected of New England medical organizations, and a prestigious employer of deeply committed professionals.

Potent Quote

"When Dr. Farber established the center fifty years ago, cancer was uniformly fatal. Today, more than half of all people can be cured, and two out of three children can lead disease-free lives."

(From the organization's web site.)

Doctors Without Borders USA, Inc.

6 East 39th Street, 8th Fl.
New York NY 10016
212/679-6800
Fax: 212/679-7016
World Wide Web: http://www.bbbsa.org/
Contact: Human Resources Department

Overview

Doctors Without Borders USA (Medecins Sans Frontieres) offers medical care to persons whose health and safety are jeopardized by natural disasters, epidemics, civil unrest, or war.

By the Numbers

Over 2,000 volunteers representing over 40 nationalities perform work in 70 nations to provide basic health care, supply vaccinations, perform surgery, upgrade medical facilities, improve sanitation and nutrition, and educate local medical staff.

The Mission

The group describes its objective as providing "medical relief to populations in crisis." It works autonomously and has no connection to governments or political, economic, or religious institutions. Voluntarism is essential to the attainment of the group's objectives.

Words to the Wise

As of this writing, the organization's web site provides information on current employment opportunities.

What to Expect

The group has gained both prominence and prestige in recent years. Although volunteer activities are central to the group's mission, paid positions do exist within Doctors Without Borders. Those considering employment in the organization should bear in mind that many of the activities undertaken by volunteers and employees involve exposure to physical danger.

Potent Quote

"Doctors Without Borders offers assistance to populations in distress, to victims of natural or man-made disasters and to victims of armed conflict, without discrimination and irrespective of race, religion, creed or political affiliation…. [M]embers are aware of the risks and dangers of the missions they undertake, and have no right to compensation for themselves or their beneficiaries other than that which Doctors Without Borders is able to afford them."

(From the organization's charter.)

Ducks Unlimited

> *1 Waterfowl Way, Memphis, Tennessee 38120*
> *1-800/45-DUCKS (453-8257)*
> *World Wide Web: http://www.ducks.org/*
> *Contact: Dave Riley*

Overview

Founded in 1937 by duck-hunting businessmen concerned about the effects of dust bowl conditions on the North American duck population, Ducks Unlimited (DU) is the world's largest private waterfowl and wetlands conservation organization. With over 550,000 members, it has worked to conserve wetlands as a means of providing sufficient breeding grounds for ducks and other waterfowl to keep them in good supply during hunting seasons. Originally begun in Washington with the absorption of a similar organization, More Game Birds, the organization now operates an office in Tennessee and has affiliates in Canada, Mexico, and New Zealand. DU often works hand in hand with state and local conservation efforts to set aside and maintain wildlife refuges, particularly in marshlands.

Over the years, DU has been instrumental in the rescue and preservation of over four million acres in Canada that provide important nesting and breeding areas for waterfowl. A similar preservation program for wintering areas was begun in Mexico in 1974. Although largely confined to the North American continent, its work is global in nature.

By the Numbers

Staff: Approximately 200.

Budget: $63,600,000.

Special events such as dinners and target shooting contests raise 46 percent of DU's funds. An additional 17 percent derives from membership dues, while 21 percent is donated by corporate sponsors (gun makers, beer companies, trucking corporations, outdoor equipment suppliers, etc.). The remainder comes from state governments, advertising in the organization's magazine, *Ducks Unlimited*, and interest. Funds are used primarily to inventory and monitor wetlands and their habitants and to purchase and develop marshland refuges for waterfowl on the North American continent. Other expenditures cover fund-raising costs, field operations, and administrative expenses.

The Mission

DU's primary objective is the preservation, protection, and management of wetlands that provide a habitat for waterfowl and other wildlife.

Words to the Wise

Twenty-five professional staff manage central headquarters; regional flyways throughout the continent are overseen by more than ninety field personnel. Competition for openings, when they arise, appears to be high.

What to Expect

Despite valiant and largely successful efforts to preserve marshlands and breeding habitats for waterfowl, Ducks Unlimited has come under sharp attack for a philosophy that also promotes hunting and the destruction of ducks and other waterfowl. The organization is best understood as a unique entity, rather than as a component of the "environmental movement." Despite criticism about its methods and aims, DU appears to be in sound financial shape and continues its vigorous conservation efforts worldwide.

Potent Quote

"DU's Governmental Affairs Office works closely with federal agencies, such as the U.S. Fish and Wildlife Service, members of Congress, and other conservation organizations. One way DU's Governmental Affairs Office helps achieve the conservation goals of the North American Waterfowl Management Plan is by aggressively seeking funding awarded under the North American Wetlands Conservation Act. Another way...is through its work with the U.S. Department of Agriculture on the Conservation Reserve Program (CRP). CRP helps reduce soil erosion and aids breeding waterfowl by providing them with safe and secure nesting habitats."

(From the organization's web site.)

Environmental Defense Fund

1875 Connecticut Avenue, NW, Washington, D.C. 20009
202/387-3500
Fax: 202-234-6049
World Wide Web: http://www.edf.org
Contact: Susan Harvey (susanh@edf.org)

Overview

The Environmental Defense Fund is one of the largest environmental organizations in the country, with over 300,000 members and branch offices in Colorado, California, North Carolina, Texas, and the District of Columbia. Through public education, research, and legislation, the EDF seeks responsible answers to environmental issues. The group works to ensure compliance with government regulations on toxic waste disposal and recycling, advocates an energy-efficiency program that reduces the burning of fossil fuels, and seeks economic solutions to environmental problems. The EDF's size, support, and strength make it one of the most powerful environmental organizations in the world.

By the Numbers

Staff: 168.

Budget: $23,500,000.

Most of EDF's income comes from membership fees, contributions, and foundation grants. Legal fees, non-foundation grants, and investment and other income make up the rest. EDF devotes 80 percent of its budget to programs and services, including education, while the remainder goes towards fund-raising and administrative costs. The organization's huge membership base gives it a solid financial foundation and testifies to strong public support of EDF's ideas, goals, and programs.

The Mission

The EDF combines scientific, economic, and legal approaches in tackling current and future environmental problems and bringing about economically viable solutions. The organization actively seeks to reform public policy on such issues as air quality, energy conservation, preservation of natural resources, land use, wildlife conservation, and control of toxic chemicals and wastes.

Words to the Wise

EDF employs a large number of full-time scientists, economists, analysts, and attorneys working on an interdisciplinary basis. Professional degrees and experience in these areas provide the best entry into the organization. Accountants, administrators, and basic office assistants are also needed. Fund-raising experience is a plus. Numerous internship opportunities are available to qualified individuals. EDF maintains many offices throughout the country; all applications for employment are processed by the Washington office (see contact information above).

A recent examination of the organization's web site yielded specific requirements for a number of professional openings in accounting, fundraising, human resources, finance, and legal areas.

What to Expect

The Environmental Defense Fund was founded by a small group of unpaid conservationists seeking to prevent the spraying of the pesticide DDT on the marshes of Long Island. This marked the first time an environment group had used the court system to address an environmental concern. The effort succeeded, and EDF went on to expand their efforts, winning a permanent, nationwide ban on DDT in 1972. EDF has since expanded into a large and highly influential organization focusing on a variety of complex environmental problems.

Today the scope of those problems may seem overwhelming—the deterioration of the ozone layer, the collapse of fisheries worldwide, and the risks posed to the planet by major climate changes. However, EDF continues its vigorous pursuit of informed and innovative solutions to ecological problems, effectively using science to influence public policy. The organization's leadership is showing increasing interest in a pragmatic approach aimed at building broad support from various constituencies. It plans to work more closely with business, community groups, property owners, and the government on environmental protection and preservation, making it easier to deliver "viable solutions" to pressing environmental problems.

Potent Quote

"New times demand new strategies. Many of the Environmental Defense Fund's early victories, and some recent ones as well, were won in court. But these days EDF is more likely to win breakthrough results by working together with businesses, government, property owners, and community groups. EDF's practical, nonpartisan, results-oriented approach for environmental protection continues to be effective both in the U.S. and abroad."

(From the 1996 Annual Report.)

Experimental Aircraft Association

> *PO Box 3086, Oshkosh, Wisconsin 54903-3086*
> *920/426-4800*
> *1-800/564-6322*
> *Fax: 920/426-4828*
> *World Wide Web: http://www.eaa.org*
> *Contact: Amy Schrader*

Overview

Since 1953, when founder Paul H. Poberezny gathered together a small group of dedicated fliers in Milwaukee, the Experimental Aircraft Association (EAA) has boasted one of the more passionate followings in the world of aviation. Through its program "Project School Flight," EEA encourages and assists industrial art classes to build various types of aircraft. It sponsors competitions, maintains an extensive library archive in aviation reference, and conducts research programs and specialized education courses focusing on aviation and aircraft building. The organization's annual meeting, held in Oshkosh, Wisconsin, attracts considerable attention not just because of the number of aircraft on display but because of the huge attendance—up to 800,000 registrants, many of whom arrive in their own planes.

EAA is affiliated with the International Aeronautical Federation and the National Aeronautic Association of the USA Through its programs and extensive membership base, it is a significant contributor to international sport aviation.

By the Numbers

The organization now boasts more than 166,000 fans of recreational flying and nearly 900 chapters worldwide, making it one of the world's largest nonprofit aviation organizations. Its annual convention (in Oshkosh, Wisconsin) has been called "the largest single aviation event in the world."

The Mission

EAA is devoted to antique and modern aircraft, the building of aircraft, and recreational flying. It seeks to make the world of flight accessible to all and to promote individual and collective achievements in flying that set standards of freedom and safety and encourage personal fulfillment in aviation pursuits. EAA works to create opportunities for its members to create and/or participate in a wide variety of programs.

Words to the Wise

EAA's paid staff is centralized at the headquarters facility in Oshkosh, Wisconsin. Its diverse and challenging job openings are often listed on the EAA web site. The organization relies heavily on its vast network of dedicated volunteers to lead and execute their programs, while its paid staff provide training, support, and back-up.

What to Expect

The human passion for aircraft and flying is not a passing phase. EAA appears likely to keep growing—and to continue catering to the needs of its exceptionally devoted members.

Potent Quote

"(Founder Paul) Poberezny taught himself to fly in a well-worn glider he rebuilt when he was sixteen years old. He racked up experience as a military pilot, but his passion for flight remained a deeply personal grassroots involvement he and his contemporaries could design and build in their garages and basements. Thus began an uninterrupted run of annual EEA fly-ins... The culture the organization serves is rightly identified as sport aviation."

(From *American Heritage*, April, 1997.)

Girl Scouts of the USA

> *420 Fifth Avenue, New York, New York 10018-2702*
> *212/852-8000*
> *World Wide Web: http://www.girlscouts.org/*
> *Contact: Janice Jacobs, Recruitment*

Overview

The Girl Scouts of the USA, founded in 1915, remains the single most popular organization in America devoted to young girls. It is also the largest voluntary organizations for girls in the world. The parent organization, which is affiliated with the World Association of Girl Guides and Girl Scouts, interacts closely with both national and international Girl Scout councils, assisting in the research, development and evaluation of programs and the training of staff and volunteers. With over three million members and a solid core of adult volunteers, the Scouting movement makes it possible for girls from all areas and backgrounds to form strong friendships, contribute to their communities, and explore their future role as women.

By the Numbers

Staff: 510.

Total income: $61,500,000.

The organization consist of 321 Girl Scout Councils within the U.S., each of which is made up of local troops chartered by the organization to administer and develop Girl Scout programs within a specified geographical area. Each Council secures its own funding to support Scouting in the local communities. Income is derived from a variety of sources, including product sales (primarily cookies and calendars), United Way support, membership fees, gifts, grants, and investments.

The Mission

Girl Scouts of the USA is aimed solely at meeting the special needs of girls, working to instill strong values and to emphasize high ideals of character, conduct, and patriotism, in order to help them become good citizens and happy, resourceful individuals. Scouting provides opportunities for girls to develop their potential and to have fun with others in a supportive, all-female environment.

Words to the Wise

Volunteerism provides the main gateway to employment with the Girl Scouts. Your dedication to Scouting goals and ideals can be demonstrated in a number of areas that can lead to a paid job, including the development and coordination of special programs, administrative assistance, consulting and advising, strategic planning, serving as liaisons with community organizations, and fund-raising. A volunteer can give as little or as much time as she likes.

What to Expect

Girl Scouting has been and will continue to be both an enjoyable outlet for girls and an activity that fulfills an important social and generational function. It has always been geared towards girls from all social and economic backgrounds and levels of physical ability. Today, the institution is adapting effectively, as it has for decades, to changing times.

In addition to providing a foundation for self-confidence and good citizenship later in life, Girl Scouting has promoted environmental protection programs and often led the way in socially relevant causes such as the fight against drug abuse, the prevention of teenage pregnancy, and the improvement of literacy among young people. This adaptability and focus on the needs of girls everywhere has made Girl Scouts of the USA a leader among organizations that serve the nation's youth. It is expected to continue to exert a strong positive influence on many future generations of girls.

Potent Quote

"The Girl Scout program has four fundamental goals that express the ways girls may benefit from their Girl Scout experiences. The four program goals for girls are: 1) To help a girl develop to her full individual potential. 2) To help a girl relate to others with increasing understanding, skill and respect. 3) To help a girl develop values to guide her actions and to provide the foundation for sound decision-making. 4) To help a girl contribute to the improvement of society through the use of her abilities and leadership skills, working in cooperation with others."

(From *Key Elements of the Girl Scout Program*.)

Goodwill Industries

> *9200 Rockville Pike, Bethesda, Maryland 20814-3896*
> *301/530-6500*
> *Fax: 301/530-1516*
> *Contact: Personnel Department*
> *World Wide Web: http://www.goodwill.org/*

Overview

In addition to helping the illiterate, the homeless, the welfare-dependent, and former criminals in becoming self-sufficient. Goodwill Industries is one of the largest nonprofit providers of employment and training services for people with disabilities. The organization's guiding principle is the belief in the power of good, honest work to transform lives. Goodwill's network of services extends through all of North America, including Canada, and reaches into thirty-seven countries besides.

By the Numbers

Goodwill's programs are largely funded through the donation of clothing and household goods, which are then sold in more than 1,500 retail stores in North America and elsewhere. Money is also raised by providing contract services to community-based businesses, as well as through fees, government grants, and monetary contributions, mostly from individuals. A small percentage of income is secured through investments.

The Mission

Goodwill Industries seeks to assist people with disabilities or special needs by helping them broaden their capabilities and by directing them to opportunities for gainful employment. These goals are accomplished through a network of community-based organizations that provide job training and employment services to the locality and throughout the world.

Words to the Wise

Information on current job opportunities may be accessed through Goodwill's web site. A recent review of the site yielded specific information on professional openings in the fields of accounting, administration, research, retail work, and data management.

What to Expect

The organization is strongly positioned to continue and expand its mission. It describes itself as "one of the world's largest nonprofit providers of employment and training services for people with disabilities and other disadvantaging conditions—such as welfare dependency, illiteracy, criminal history and homelessness." Goodwill Industries' continuing dedication to broadening its mission is little short of remarkable.

Potent Quote

"Goodwill Industries will actively strive to achieve the full participation in society of people with disabilities and other individuals with special needs by expanding their opportunities and occupational capabilities through a network of autonomous, nonprofit, community-based organizations providing services throughout the world in response to local needs."

(From the organization's mission statement.)

Greenpeace

> *1436 U Street, NW, Washington, D.C. 20009*
> *202/462-1177*
> *Fax: 202/462-4507*
> *Job Line: 202/319-2500*
> *World Wide Web: http://www.greenpeaceusa.org*
> *Contact: T. Webb, Human Resources*

Overview

Greenpeace is an internationally renowned organization focusing on such environmental issues as the elimination of toxic waste, the protection and preservation of oceans and marine life, saving the ozone layer, finding alternative energy sources, and nuclear disarmament. The organization uses a number of different avenues, including public education, canvassing, and grassroots lobbying, to achieve its goals. It also publishes a large number of books, newsletters, and media materials to advance public knowledge of environmental concerns. Headquartered in Washington, Greenpeace also maintains offices in New York, San Francisco, Seattle, and Chicago. It is a large, volunteer-driven organization that maintains its independence from any political party or partisan stance on issues. Its remarkable growth since its founding in 1971 has vividly demonstrated its major impact on the public perception of ecological issues now affecting the world.

By the Numbers

Staff: 175 full-time; 500 summer employees (canvassers).

Budget: $42,800,000.

Greenpeace does not accept any government funding. Direct-mail campaigns draw in 44 percent of Greenpeace's income, with canvassing bringing an additional 31 percent. Major donors and merchandise sales account for 14 percent of income, while the remaining 11 percent is gained from telephone solicitations. Programs and services receive 86 percent of the annual budget, the remainder going into fundraising efforts and administrative costs. Through the Greenpeace Fund, grants are awarded to a network of Greenpeace affiliates in thirty-one countries, and support is given to extensive research in ecological issues.

The Mission

Through educational, research, and outreach programs, Greenpeace aims to preserve the world's environment and protect it for future generations. The organization's stated purpose is "to create a green and peaceful world." It achieves its mission largely by the process of "bearing witness"—that is, publicizing environmental abuse by their resolute and non-violent presence at the scene of the abuse.

Words to the Wise

The best route into the organization is by becoming a canvasser. Greenpeace currently has 25 canvass offices throughout the country. There is also a need for campaigners, managers, fund raisers, and administrative staff, in addition to numerous specialty positions. Jobs are advertised via newspapers, postings on college campuses, and mailings to related organizations. Volunteerism also provides an avenue into Greenpeace.

What to Expect

Greenpeace USA recently suffered a drop in support, from 4.8 million members in 1990 to something more than 3 million members in 1996. The organization suffered financial setbacks in the early 1990s, but the financial picture has become more stable since Executive Director Barbara Dudley took over the reins in 1993. Although still successful in its mission, the organization has been criticized for what some see as succumbing to institutionalization, taking it away from the cutting edge of environmental activism and reform. Critics have also complained about the high salaries paid to some Greenpeace executives. These factors have led to a series of important and still unresolved questions on leadership, organization, and direction. The organization continues to score major successes, however, in its fight to win public attention and support for environmental issues.

Potent Quote

"In 1971, a small but determined crew made its way slowly through the cold North Pacific waters off Alaska aboard the Phyllis Cormack, an aging 80-foot halibut seiner. They were members of the Don't Make a Wave Committee, now known worldwide as Greenpeace. And they were ready to put their lives on the line to protest nuclear weapons tests planned for Amchitka Island. This brave voyage was the beginning of many successful actions to save our planet.... The history of Greenpeace is the story of its campaigns, the actions that have typified many of them, their success in bringing about change, and Greenpeace's own expansion in terms of its supporters, revenues, national offices, staff and fleet."

(From the organization's web site.)

Guggenheim Museum

1071 Fifth Avenue, New York, New York 10128
212/423-3500
Fax: 212/423-3640
World Wide Web: http://www.guggenheim.org/srgm.html
Contact: Human Resources Department

Overview

The Solomon R. Guggenheim Museum in New York houses what is considered to be one of the great collections of modern and contemporary art in the world. The building itself, designed by Frank Lloyd Wright, completed in 1959 (only six months after the great architect's death) remains both striking and unique after nearly four decades. It is held by many to be one of the museum's own greatest holdings. Thousands upon thousands of visitors from all over the world visit the Guggenheim annually.

By the Numbers

Staff: Over 100.

The museum engages in a variety of income-generating activities. The institution is actually an international museum—the only one in the world—made up of three branches—the famous Wright structure on Fifth Avenue, the Guggenheim Museum SoHo, and the Peggy Guggenheim Collection in Venice.

The Mission

The Guggenheim is one of the country's leading art museums, with a major focus on modern painting and sculpture.

Words to the Wise
The Guggenheim hires twenty full-time interns a year to help research and prepare exhibitions, and to do some clerical work. Summer internships occasionally include a small stipend.

What to Expect
Those applying for internships (and presumably for full-time positions) are expected to be deeply interested in the arts, preferably with an educational background to match.

Potent Quote
"The Guggenheim Museum has one of the world's largest collections of Kandinsky, as well as major holdings of works by Brancusi, Calder, Chagall, Delaunay, Klee, Miro, Picasso, and many other artists of this century. The collection was founded during the late 1920s by Solomon R. Guggenheim with the assistance of his art adviser, Hill Rebay. Inspired by Rebay's commitment to abstract painting, Guggenheim began collecting in Europe and America. In 1937 he set up the Solomon R. Guggenheim foundation with the specific purpose of creating a museum…. In 1976, Justin K. Thannhauser, one of the great collectors of the modern era, bequeathed masterworks by Cezanne, Degas, Gauguin, Manet, Picasso, Toulouse-Lautrec, and others to the museum."

(From the organization's web site.)

Habitat for Humanity International

> *121 Habitat Street, Americus, Georgia 31709-3498*
> *912/924-6935*
> *World Wide Web: http://www.habitat.org/*
> *Contact: Cheryl Caldwell, Human Resources*

Overview

Habitat for Humanity has achieved fame not only for its achievements in building affordable housing, but also for its best-known volunteer, former President Jimmy Carter. Since its founding in 1976, Habitat has been responsible for the construction of more than twenty thousand homes; its reach now extends beyond U.S. boundaries. The organization is linked in partnership to people in over forty countries, more than a thousand cities in all. Affiliates work to build low-income housing in the U.S. and abroad, including Asia, Africa, and Latin America. Habitat also sponsors educational programs to emphasize the importance of quality, affordable housing everywhere.

By the Numbers

Staff: Approximately 290.

Budget: $21,000,000.

Funding for Habitat for Humanity is provided by churches and foundations, as well as through tax-deductible contributions from corporations and individuals. It does not accept government funding for construction, renovation, or repair purposes; however, it will use government funds for the acquisition of land or houses requiring renovations. Donations are used according to the express wishes of the donor. Programs and services account for 72 percent of expenditures; 20 percent goes into fundraising efforts, and the remainder is devoted to publications, educational efforts, and administrative costs.

Habitat for Humanity relies heavily on volunteer labor as a means of cutting costs. Completed Habitat houses are sold without profit to approved homeowners and are financed with no-interest loans. Monthly mortgage payments are then recycled back into a revolving fund (the Fund for Humanity), the monies from which are used to help build more houses.

The Mission

Habitat for Humanity works to build and renovate affordable, decent houses for people in need, and by so doing to eliminate poverty and homelessness. It is an ecumenical Christian organization dedicated to the proposition that decent housing in good communities is a means by which people can live according to God's word and promise.

Words to the Wise

Habitat for Humanity is a service-oriented program, and as such relies largely on unpaid volunteer efforts. However, some positions are paid at either an hourly rate or, depending on the nature and location of the work, at a $25.00-per-week stipend plus lodging, or $300 a month plus lodging. Paid staff positions range from organizers and coordinators to office staff and managers. There are about ten to fifteen job openings a year, most of which are advertised in the bimonthly magazine, *Habitat World,* and other publications.

What to Expect

The organization's work has received a great deal of positive media attention in recent years. Habitat for Humanity seems likely to continue to expand its efforts on behalf of affordable housing.

Potent Quote

"Homeowners invest hundreds of hours of their own labor—'sweat equity'—into building their Habitat house and the houses of others. Sweat equity reduces the monetary cost of the house, increases the personal stake of the family members in their house, and fosters the development of partnerships with other people in the community. The amount and type of sweat equity required of each partner family vary from affiliate to affiliate. Three hundred to five hundred hours per family is common."

(From the organization's web site.)

Harvard University

17 Quincy Street, Cambridge, Massachusetts 02138
617/495-2771
World Wide Web: http://www.hr.harvard.edu/employment/
Contact: Human Resources

Overview

Harvard University was founded a mere sixteen years after the Pilgrims landed in North America, making it the oldest institution for higher education in the country. The University currently enrolls close to 19,000 undergraduate and graduate degree candidates from approximately 120 countries. In addition, the Harvard Extension School has an average enrollment of 13,000 students. The University maintains the largest university library in the world, with more than twelve million books and innumerable other materials and databases, and collections in 90 other libraries in Boston, Cambridge, Washington, D.C., and Florence, Italy.

By the Numbers

Staff: 12,000.

Rich in land and holdings, the University at the end of fiscal 1994 had an endowment estimated at more than $6.2 billion.

The Mission

Harvard University is a private educational institution providing degree programs in the liberal arts, business, design, divinity, education, government, law, medicine, public health, and dentistry. In addition to its undergraduate program it has ten graduate and professional schools.

Words to the Wise

Questions concerning employment openings may be forwarded to the Human Resource office in Cambridge.

What to Expect

Harvard is one of the country's most prestigious—and wealthiest—educational institutions. It is also among the most stable of the nation's bodies of higher learning. Many of the positions for which it interviews applicants are highly competitive.

Potent Quote

"The Employment Office posts all open positions and provides information on the hiring processes at Harvard University. While this page contains a great deal of the information we offer, including the open job listings, we encourage you to stop by our office at 11 Holyoke Street, Cambridge, MA 02138 if you would like more information about finding a job at Harvard."

(From the organization's web site.)

Human Rights Watch

> *485 Fifth Avenue*
> *New York, NY 10017-6104*
> *212/972-8400*
> *Fax: 212/972-0905*
> *World Wide Web: http://www.hrw.org/*
> *Contact: "Directors of individual regions."*
> *(New York office can provide information on the office nearest you.)*

Overview

Human Rights Watch is an international human rights advocacy organizations active in Africa, the Americas, Europe and the former Soviet Union, and the Middle East.

By the Numbers

The group is organized according to 5 regional international divisions and 3 "thematic projects" (Arms, Children's rights, and Women's Rights). It maintains U.S. offices in New York, Los Angeles, and Washington, D.C. The organization's web site also lists 5 "areas of special initiative": human rights in the U.S., prisons, free expression, business and human rights, anti-narcotics campaigns and human rights, and academic freedom.

The Mission

The group is strongly focused on identifying, publicizing, and preventing human rights abuses, and on "hold[ing] abusers accountable."

Words to the Wise

As of this writing, the organization's web site provides information on current employment opportunities.

What to Expect

The group remains vigorous and active in the pursuit of its mission. Applicants should be aware that some openings entail overseas work.

Potent Quote

"Human Rights Watch is dedicated to protecting the human rights of people around the world. We stand with victims and activists to prevent discrimination, to uphold political freedom, to protect people from inhumane conduct in wartime, and to bring offenders to justice."

(From the organization's web site.)

The Hunger Project

> *15 East 26th Street*
> *New York NY 10010*
> *212/251-9100*
> *World Wide Web: http://www.thp.org/*
> *Contact: Personnel Department*

Overview

The organization works to eradicate hunger globally, taking as a given that the international community "possesses the financial and technical resources necessary" to accomplish this goal.

By the Numbers

Total revenues and other support: $5,000,000.

In addition to the Global Office in New York, The Hunger Project operates nine international offices. Three designated global regions (India, Bangladesh, and Africa) have been the focus of Strategic Planning-in-Action campaigns, resulting in "breakthroughs in health, education, food production, nutrition, the empowerment of women, and improved incomes."

Words to the Wise

Questions concerning employment openings may be forwarded to the New York office.

What to Expect

Deeply committed to resolving the problem of hunger on a global basis, the Hunger Project has been increasingly effective at winning support for its work. Revenues from contributions and other sources appear to be on the rise.

Potent Quote

"One-third of the world's remaining hunger is in India. In India, our work began with a partnership with the Planning Commission, starting with a national strategy conference in November 1990. The Hunger Project received a mandate to pioneer a new approach, which became known as Strategic Planning-in-Action (SPIA). SPIA is today being implemented in ten states of India.... The current emphasis is the creation of hunger-free zones—designated, large-scale areas (100,000 to 1 million people) where hunger will be completely eradicated. Hunger-free zones are currently being created in twenty-two districts."

(From the organization's web site.)

The Hemlock Society

P.O. Box 101810, Denver, Colorado 80250-1810
303/639-1202
1-800/247-7421
Fax: 303/639-1224
World Wide Web: http://www2.privatei.com/hemlock/
Contact: Jonathan Bennett-Scott

Overview

The Hemlock Society is one of the foremost advocates of self-determination in decisions affecting the termination of life. The Society seeks through public education and publications to create a more accepting climate for those terminally ill, mentally competent individuals who choose to end their own lives—and for the physicians who assist them. The organization addresses this emotional and morally difficult issue in a variety of ways.

The Hemlock Society organizes conferences, provides a clearinghouse for legal information and publications on the right to die, offers intervention and referral services, and assists in the development and support of local chapters throughout the U.S. Its political arm is the Patient's Rights Organization (PRO-USA), whose aim is to change the law in all fifty states to allow for physician assistance in dying for the terminally ill.

By the Numbers

The Hemlock Society has 25,000 members across the country, organized into 80 chapters and community groups. The group reports that it responds to an average of 1,000 calls a month requesting information on death and dying. It also publishes a quarterly magazine (*TimeLines*) and a monthly magazine (*Chapter Leader Resource*).

The Mission

Through education and research, The Hemlock Society seeks to influence public understanding and acceptance of the right to self-determination for all end-of-life decisions. The Society believes that terminally ill people must be able to make their own decisions regarding death in a way that enables them to preserve their personal integrity, self-respect, and dignity. To this end, the Society also wishes to instill public and legal acceptance of the physician's role in assisting mentally competent, dying individuals to a peaceful end. The group does not encourage suicide, but does believe that the final decision to terminate life is a deeply personal, individual one.

Words to the Wise

Questions concerning employment openings may be forwarded to the Denver office.

What to Expect

Hemlock's mission is often perceived as a controversial one, but the organization's members have come to rely on its many resources, and the issue of the right to a "good death" is likely to be a matter of public policy debate for some time to come.

Potent Quote

"The Hemlock Society USA has initiated a national Patient Advocacy Program in which medical and legal staff are available on a 24-hour basis to intervene for any Hemlock member whose advance directive is being ignored or who is in excessive pain which is not being treated. A dedicated Advocacy phone line is available for access and an advisory panel of doctors, nurses, physicians and mental health professionals will also work with the Advocacy program."

(From the organization's web site.)

Henry J. Kaiser Family Foundation

2400 Sand Hill Road, Menlo Park, California 94025
415/854-9400
Fax: 415/854-4800
or
1450 G Street, NW, Suite 250, Washington, D.C. 20005
202/347-5270
Fax: 202/347-5274
World Wide Web: http://www.kff.org/
Contact: Dr. Diane Rowland

Overview

The grants awarded by the Henry J. Kaiser Family Foundation cover a wide range of programs and activities in the area of health care, including the analysis of public policy, research into public health problems, initiation of pilot projects, and activities in communication to stimulate public debate on health care. While the Foundation supports grantees in other states and South Africa, a large part of its focus has been on its own home state of California and issues of public policy and health care reform there.

By the Numbers

Staff: Approximately 30.

In a recent year, the fund disbursed approximately $23 million in grants.

The Mission

The Henry J. Kaiser Family Foundation is a philanthropic organization that provides grants to other organizations and programs aimed at improving the quality of health care, particularly as it affects low-income and minority groups.

Words to the Wise

Although the organization may be of significant interest to those interested in pursuing opportunities involving health care and poverty issues, openings, when they arise, are likely to be highly competitive.

What to Expect

The foundation, established in 1948, is stable and well respected. The quality of managed health care in the country today is a point of particular concern to many Americans. The Kaiser Family Foundation's work helps to ensure that legitimate public concerns in this area are addressed fairly and responsibly.

Potent Quote

"The Foundation's work is focused on four main areas: health policy, reproductive health, HIV policy, and health and development in South Africa. The Foundation also maintains a special interest in health policy and innovation in its home state of California."

(From the organization's web site.)

International Rescue Committee (IRC)

> *122 East 42nd Street, New York, New York 10168*
> *212/551-3000*
> *Fax: 212/551-3180*
> *Job Hotline: 212/551-3190*
> *World Wide Web: http://www.intrescom.org/*
> *Contact: Louise Shea, Vice President of Human Resources;*
> *Monique Thormann, Regional Recruitment Officer;*
> *Susan Riehl, Regional Recruitment Officer;*
> *Andrew Roberts, Emergency Recruiter*
> *(depending on region and job opportunity being offered)*

Overview

The International Rescue Committee was established in 1933 at the request of Albert Einstein to aid refugees from Hitler's campaign of terror in Germany. Today it remains active in providing assistance to refugees from war, oppression, and political, ethnic, or religious persecution. Currently the IRC runs assistance and service programs in more than twenty countries, making it the world's foremost nonprofit, nonsectarian volunteer organization dedicated to rescue, relief, and rehabilitation. It has earned a well-deserved international reputation as a "good guy."

By the Numbers

Staff: 397.

Total income from recent year: $76,500,000.

The majority of the Committee's income is invested in relief programs and services in Africa, Asia, Europe, the former Soviet Union, and the United States of America, with only about 7 percent set aside for fundraising and administration. The IRC's paid staff is governed by a board of directors who work without compensation. A spirit of volunteerism pervades the organization.

The Mission
The IRC works throughout the world to aid victims and refugees of war, violence, famine, persecution, and totalitarian oppression. Through resettlement assistance, emergency relief, rehabilitation, and advocacy efforts, the Committee strives to win freedom, human dignity, and self-reliance for these victims and refugees.

Words to the Wise
The IRC maintains operations in at least fifteen countries around the world, in addition to many offices within the United States. Persons combining bilingual or multilingual capabilities with administrative, public health, or income-generating experience are the likeliest prospects for employment with the Committee. Other job requirements would be dependent on the specific projects or needs within the region being served. Call for information or visit the IRC's web site for more details on employment opportunities in Africa, Asia, Europe, the United States, and the New York headquarters.

What to Expect
The IRC's rescue efforts are more important and relevant today than ever. Recent campaigns to help victims and refugees in regions torn by strife have brought humanitarian aid and rehabilitation assistance to the former Yugoslavia, Bosnia, Rwanda, and the republics of the former Soviet Union. Its network of agencies provides innumerable services around the planet, bringing self-sufficiency to people in their own countries and resettlement and job opportunities to those who cannot return to the lands of their birth. The need for the organization's rescue work is likely to remain strong.

Potent Quote

"IRC staff and volunteers work in Africa, Asia, Europe, the former Soviet Republics, and the United States. A unique ability to respond quickly to refugee emergencies has marked the International Rescue committee's history. It was founded in 1933, at the request of Albert Einstein, to assist [those] fleeing Hitler's terror. Over the past six years, IRC has tripled in size."

(From the organization's web site.)

Isabella Stewart Gardner Museum

280 The Fenway, Boston MA 02115
Mailing address 2 Palace Road, Boston MA 02115
617/566-1401
World Wide Web: http://www.boston.com/gardner/
Contact: Joanne Gormley, Human Resources

Overview

The Isabella Stewart Gardner Museum is one of the premier museums in New England—and the only major museum in the United States (and perhaps the world) in which the collection and the building that houses it are the work of a single individual.

A gift to Boston from one of its wealthiest citizens, Isabella Stewart Gardner, the museum, which was opened to the public in 1903, is something of a time capsule. Mrs. Gardner herself designed the building to be a showplace for her collection. Her will stipulates that the museum must never undergo any alteration, and that all of the objects in it—paintings, sculpture, drawings, prints, furniture, textiles, ceramics, glass, etc.—must remain exactly as Mrs. Gardner left them. Since the widely reported theft of several masterworks of painting in 1990, the walls remain bare in the spots where the works were hung.

By the Numbers

The museum contains approximately 2,500 works of art, and draws 175,000 visitors annually.

The Mission

The Museum seeks to carry out the instructions left by its founder and to provide a means for the public to experience and learn from the remarkable Gardner collection.

Words to the Wise
Questions about current employment openings may be forwarded to the Boston office.

What to Expect
The organization was left amply endowed by Mrs. Gardner, and it remains in good financial health. As explained under "Overview," future expansion is an impossibility.

Potent Quote
The Museum was left by its founder for "the education and enjoyment of the public forever."

(From museum press materials.)

Jane Goodall Institute

P.O. Box 599, Ridgefield CT 06877
203/431-2099
Fax: 203/431-4387
World Wide Web: http://www.wcsu.ctstateu.edu/cyberchimp
Contact: Personnel Department

Overview

Named for renowned primate researcher Jane Goodall, the Jane Goodall Institute (JGI) is devoted to wildlife research, education, and conservation—and to Goodall's special interest, the chimpanzee. Operating on the principle that the chimpanzee is, like the human animal, a part of the complex tapestry of life, the Institute focuses special attention on the chimp because of its unique status as a) the closest relative to man and b) an endangered species. Programs devoted to research, education, and long-term preservation are the Institute's highest priority. They include research centers and zoo projects, lectures, newsletters, merchandise sales, and specially designed educational activities. The Goodall Institute also focuses attention on environmental issues that affect the chimpanzee and its habitat through such programs as reforestation projects and animal sanctuaries.

By the Numbers

The Institute is supported largely through member donations. One important avenue for fundraising involves encouraging members to become Chimp Guardians. That means their donations will be devoted to a specific chimp in JGI's care. All donations are applied to food, shelter, and medical supplies in the sanctuaries.

The Mission

The Jane Goodall Institute has a four-part mission, focused primarily on chimpanzees. First and foremost, the Institute promotes research of primates, and specifically of chimpanzees, both in natural and in captive environments. Second, educational methods are applied to increase international awareness about chimpanzees and other environmental issues. Third, the Institute seeks to ensure the long-term survival and preservation of chimpanzees in the wild through the implementation of conservation activities. Finally, the Institute works to ensure that all animals, but most especially chimpanzees, remain physically and psychologically secure in both wild and captive (i.e., sanctuary) environments.

Words to the Wise

Questions about employment opportunities may be forwarded to the Ridgefield address.

What to Expect

Thanks in large measure to the renown of its founder, the JGI is now stable and well positioned for the future. The Institute recently expanded, establishing another center, the Jane Goodall Center for Excellence in Environmental Studies, as a partnership between the JGI and Western Connecticut State University. This new center will offer interdisciplinary programs for students, educators, and the community at large, and will work to create greater awareness and understanding of environmental issues. The JGI also works to create programs that involve young people in the conservation movement, especially chimpanzee conservation. This latest expansion of the organization's efforts reflects a pattern of growth that may increase future employment opportunities within the organization.

Potent Quote

"[The new Jane Goodall Center for Excellence in Environmental Studies] will link the extraordinary resources of The Jane Goodall Institute with Western Connecticut State University's long-standing commitment to teacher education and community outreach."

(From the organization's web site.)

La Frontera Center, Inc.

502 West 29th Street, Tucson, Arizona 85713-3394
520/884-9920, ext. 424 (Job Line)
Fax: 520/792-0654
Contact: Human Resources

Overview

Founded in 1968, La Frontera Center is the largest provider of comprehensive services in behavioral health in the state of Arizona. The Center
emphasizes a strong program in vocational rehabilitation and also provides therapeutic day care services. Other programs include counseling
services for individuals and families, residential substance abuse services for adults, and housing assistance for the homeless and mentally
ill. The Center provides mental health services to adults and children on
an outpatient basis and offers assistance to victims of domestic violence.
Overall, La Frontera Center provides invaluable widespread assistance
to a large constituency based largely in Pima County and Southern Arizona. It is one of the premier programs of its kind in the country.

By the Numbers

Staff: 250.

Budget: $11,000,000.

Contracts account for 80 percent of La Frontera Center's funding. Foundations provide another 15 percent, and individual contributions make
up the rest.

The Mission

La Frontera Center responds to the needs of a culturally diverse community by providing a network of services in mental health, substance

abuse, homelessness, domestic violence, and rehabilitation in numerous areas.

Words to the Wise

There may be up to twenty-five staff openings a year. The greatest need is likely to be for counselors, therapists, and specialists in vocational rehabilitation. Openings also arise for day care providers and office workers. Part-time employees, volunteers, and interns are all accepted. Jobs are advertised through local papers and a job line, in addition to internal postings.

What to Expect

The organization's work with members of its service community is likely to be emotionally demanding, but highly rewarding for those motivated to pursue it.

Potent Quote

"[La Frontera Center is a] community behavioral health center offering individual, family, and group counseling; substance abuse services for children, adults, and families; and psychological rehabilitation services for adults diagnosed as seriously mentally ill... including outpatient vocational rehabilitation, partial hospitalization programs, and long-term or transitional housing."

(From Tucson's "Information and Referral Services" summary.)

Lahey Hitchcock Clinic

> *41 Mall Road, Burlington, Massachusetts 01805*
> *781/306-1003 (Job line)*
> *World Wide Web: http://www.lahey.hitchcock.org/*
> *Contact: Human Resources*

Overview

The Lahey Hitchcock Clinic was formed in January 1995, when the Lahey Clinic of Massachusetts and the Hitchcock Clinic of New Hampshire and Vermont joined forces to create a health care network of more than 960 physicians, covering every specialty and subspecialty of medicine. The cornerstones of the Clinic are the Lahey Hitchcock Medical Center in Burlington, Massachusetts (272 beds) and the Dartmouth-Hitchcock Medical Center located in Lebanon, New Hampshire (429 beds). The Lahey-Hitchcock network also includes health centers for primary and secondary care in Arlington and Peabody, Massachusetts, and in Concord, Keene, Manchester, and Nashua, New Hampshire.

By the Numbers

Staff: 6,924.

There are 15 community-based practices in the western and North Shore suburbs of Boston, and more than 50 community-based practices throughout New Hampshire and Vermont.

The Mission

Lahey Hitchcock Clinic provides primary care health services on a community basis, as well as specialty-care services in medical centers throughout Massachusetts, new Hampshire, and Vermont. A major part of its mission involves an emphasis on education and research, which it pursues through its affiliations with Dartmouth Medical School and

Tufts University School of Medicine, and through training programs for medical residents and fellows.

Words to the Wise

The Clinic offers numerous opportunities in a variety of areas, including medicine, nursing, allied health, administrative support, information systems, technical support, and other services. Job openings are advertised in newspapers and professional journals, and opportunities may also be accessed via on-line job postings on the organization's web site.

What to Expect

The organization is stable and well positioned for the future attainment of its goals.

Potent Quote

"Lahey Hitchcock Clinic offers educational programs, health screenings, medical check-ups and access to high-quality primary and specialty care under one umbrella."

(From the organization's web site.)

The League of Women Voters

1730 M St., NW, Washington, D.C. 20036-4508
202/429-1965
Fax: 202/429-0854
World Wide Web: http://www.lwv.org/
Contact: Joan Luedtki

Overview

Founded in 1920, the League of Women Voters (LWV) is a nationwide, multi-issue group seeking to promote the informed and active participation of citizens in government. The organization also pursues a variety of education and advocacy goals.

The League is open to both men and women. It is strictly nonpartisan and does not support particular parties or candidates. It does, however, assume positions on selected issues, such as gun control, reproductive choice, and full voter representation.

By the Numbers

The group is organized in more than 1,000 communities nationally, and in all 50 states and the Virgin Islands.

The Mission

The League of Women Voters describes its mission as twofold: encouraging citizen participation in, and understanding of, government; and promoting public policies that support the organization's goals. The LWV's Education Fund "furnishes impartial, accurate information on which the American people depend to make informed decision on a range of public policy issues."

Words to the Wise
Questions concerning employment openings may be forwarded to the Washington office.

What to Expect
The group has a historic dedication to "open governmental systems," especially as expressed in fair election processes, voting rights and access advocacy, and campaign reform initiatives. The League secured an important victory in 1993 with the passage of national voter registration reform legislation. Current media coverage of campaign finance reform issues suggests that this topic, one of deep and abiding interest to the League, will continue to occupy a prominent position on the national agenda.

Potent Quote

"We: *act* after study and member agreement to achieve solutions in the public interest on key community issues at all government levels; *build* citizen participation in the democratic process; *engage* communities in promoting positive solutions to public policy issues through education and advocacy. We believe in respect for individuals, the value of diversity, the empowerment of the grassroots (both within the League and in communities), [and] the power of collective decision making for the common good. We will act with trust, integrity, and professionalism."

(From the organization's web site.)

Make-a-Wish Foundation of America

100 West Clarendon Avenue, Suite 2200, Phoenix, Arizona 85013-3518
800/722-WISH (9474)
Fax: 602/279-0855
World Wide Web: http://www.wish.org/
Contact: June Fessenden

Overview

Make-a-Wish Foundation's devotion to fulfilling the wishes of children with terminal illnesses has elicited widespread admiration—and a number of imitators. Established in 1983, the Foundation encourages the development of chapters everywhere and helps to generate donations for chapter organizations, for which it also provides marketing support, training, and policy/governance services from its headquarters in Phoenix. In addition, it creates training programs and workshops designed to assist in the development of programs and goals within the individual chapters. With thirteen affiliates in other nations, Make-a-Wish is the largest and most respected organization of its kind in the world.

By the Numbers

Staff: 32 paid staff; 80 volunteers;
     81 affiliate organizations with over 11,000 volunteers.

Budget: $4,600,000.

Make-a-Wish is a privately funded grass-roots organization. It is financed by contributions from individuals, corporations, and foundations, in addition to chapter fees and assessments. All but 10 percent of its income goes to programs and services for children and to training and education. The remainder is devoted to fund-raising and administration costs. On average, it costs $3,500 to fulfill each child's wish. In the fiscal year ending August 31, 1996, Make-a-Wish volunteers in the U.S. granted nearly 6,500 wishes.

The Mission

Make-a-Wish was founded specifically to fulfill the special wishes of children under eighteen years of age who are terminally ill or have a life-threatening illness that makes it probable that the child will not survive beyond the age of eighteen. Since its inception, Make-a-Wish has granted over 50,000 wishes for children around the world.

Words to the Wise

Competition for paid employment can be heavy. Make-a-Wish relies almost exclusively on its network of volunteers to carry out wish fulfillments, provide administrative and office support, and cover fund-raising, public relations, and legal assistance.

What to Expect

From the very first wish granted to a dying boy in Phoenix that inspired the formation of the Foundation, Make-a-Wish has grown into the largest wish-granting organization in the world. It is fueled by generous public support and the dedicated work of its volunteers. Its success and popularity, and its ever-present clientele of terminally ill children, has ensured that it will continue to grow and fulfill millions of wishes in the years ahead.

The fulfillment of children's wishes can create special moments of joy and magic for all involved, despite the often tragic circumstances that may surround the activity. The work can be deeply satisfying and provides a special kind of reward—that of helping a terminally ill child.

At the same time, the organization's work carries an equal measure of sadness. Most of the children for whom wishes are granted will die, and some who survive their illness may be permanently ill or incapacitated. For employees and volunteers, emotional distress can be a danger if proper care is not taken to handle the lows that may accompany the work.

Potent Quote

"The Make-A-Wish Foundation represents one of the most worthwhile efforts in the nonprofit sector. After seventeen years of outstanding accomplishments, we have a tremendous opportunity to move to a greater level of service in granting the wishes of eligible children on a global scale."

(From the organization's web site.)

Massachusetts General Hospital Corporation/Partners HealthCare

55 Fruit Street, Boston, Massachusetts 02114
617/724-2266
World Wide Web: http://www.mgh.harvard.edu/
Contact: Office of Recruitment

Overview

The General Hospital Corporation is the chief operating arm of Massachusetts General Hospital, in affiliation with Partners HealthCare Systems, Inc. The largest teaching hospital within the Harvard Medical School system, Mass. General offers short-term acute care, with a nine hundred-bed facility providing the latest in diagnostic and therapeutic care in various specialties and subspecialties of medicine. The oldest and largest hospital in New England, Massachusetts General Hospital (MGH or "Mass. General") has a tradition of excellence and is consistently ranked as one of the finest teaching hospitals in the U.S. It maintains professional affiliations with numerous other hospitals and health care clinics in the Greater Boston area.

By the Numbers

Staff: 13,000.

Budget: $750,000,000.

MGH conducts the largest hospital-based research program in the United States, receiving more funds from the National Institutes of Health than any other independent U.S. hospital. In 1997, hospital admissions and out-patient visits rose significantly while other hospitals in the region were being forced to shrink or even close. As a result of its formation of Partners HealthCare System with the Brigham and

Women's Hospital, Mass. General is in the soundest financial shape ever, projecting a net gain of about $4.6 million for FY 1997.

The Mission

Massachusetts General Hospital works to provide the highest-quality health care to the community and to individual patients. It also seeks to promote scientific research in the cause of improved medical care, and to educate and train the health care leaders of the future.

Words to the Wise

Massachusetts General Hospital provides many employment opportunities in professional health care and in administrative and other support. Because of its research component, scientists are frequently sought. The Hospital offers numerous training and career development opportunities, as well as summer internships and work-study programs. Job opportunities are always available in many diverse areas and are advertised in local newspapers and in professional journals, along with the usual internal postings.

The hospital provides for a varied and interesting work culture. A diverse staff reflects the Hospital's commitment to equal-opportunity employment. The Hospital also offers a tuition reimbursement program, one way in which it encourages personal and career development for employees. A large number of the professional staff become mentors to younger colleagues, making for a supportive work environment.

What to Expect

In March, 1994, MGH merged with the Brigham & Women's Hospital to form Partners HealthCare System, Inc. This alliance was created in order to provide a better, more cost-effective health care delivery system while maintaining the historic dedication of both hospitals to teaching and research. As the health care industry has changed in response to technological advances and the varied needs of its clientele, MGH has changed as well, adapting in order to provide the best possible service.

It has recently moved to form an alliance in cancer care with the Dana-Farber Cancer Institute, to create better approaches to patient care with its affiliated hospitals, and to improve collaboration efforts in research and teaching with the Harvard Medical School. The MGH is currently in solid financial health. Its influence as one of the world's preeminent teaching and research hospitals will remain constant and on the cutting edge of biomedical advances.

Although it is a huge employer, Mass. General offers a very personal and friendly work environment for its employees, with plenty of support provided for personal growth and career development. There is a sense of community within many departments, and employees are frequently recognized for their achievements through in-house newsletters and ceremonies such as the annual Ether Day celebration. Staff also enjoy the advantage and prestige of working for a worldwide leader in modern health care and biomedical research.

In recent years, as the hospital has responded to the financial challenges of modern health care delivery, it has reduced many of the once-substantial benefits it offered to employees. Salary increases may be minimal, and wages may even be frozen for periods of time—an important consideration for those who associate size with increased career growth. In fact, the sheer scale of the organization may be off-putting to someone who prefers a more intimate working environment.

Potent Quote

"To provide the highest quality care to individuals and to the community, to advance care through excellence in biomedical research, and to educate future academic and practice leaders of the health care professions."

(From the organization's mission statement.)

Massachusetts Half-Way Houses, Inc.

PO Box 348, Back Bay Annex, Boston, MA 02117
617/482-2520
Contact: Human Resources Manager

Overview

Through the use of human services, training programs and technical assistance, Massachusetts Half-Way Houses, Inc. (MHHI) has successfully helped integrate ex-convicts back into the community. The organization has expanded into similar integration services for the mentally retarded with the establishment of Community Strategies.

By the Numbers

Staff: 118.

Budget: $4,500,000.

Public contracts provide 85 percent of the organization's funding; the remainder comes from foundations and individual contributions.

The Mission

MHHI assists ex-offenders (men, women, adults, and juveniles) who are newly out of prison or detention by providing them with support services on both a residential and non-residential basis.

Words to the Wise

MHHI seems to experience a fairly high turnover, resulting in up to twenty-four staff openings a year. Most of these are for caseworkers (sixty-seven positions in all), who are supported by an executive and office staff. Salaries tend to be relatively low. MHHI also relies on volunteers to assist, and interns are accepted and paid on a work-study basis.

What to Expect

The counseling work performed by MHHI counselors, while likely to be in demand for some time to come, can be draining and stressful. For the right person, however, working with the organization can carry significant emotional rewards.

Potent Quote

"[The organization's goal is] achieving successful reintegration into the community after incarceration."

(MHHI press materials.)

The Massachusetts Public Interest Research Group (MASSPIRG)

29 Temple Place, Boston MA 02111
617/292-4800
Fax: 292-8057
Contact: Lisa Bernstein, Assistant Hiring Director
World Wide Web: http://www.igc.apc.org/pirg/masspirg/

Overview

MASSPIRG is a public interest organization that safeguards citizens' interests through its monitoring of government activities. The group conducts research and lobbies governmental bodies on behalf of Massachusetts consumers, providing a strong and effective advocacy for environmental and consumer issues. The voting records of representatives are also monitored and documented for MASSPIRG members. Believing that government is accountable to the people, MASSPIRG lobbies for a clean environment, the preservation of natural resources, and strong consumer protections. It is a large and influential part of the environmental movement in the region.

By the Numbers

MASSPIRG is funded largely by member donations.

As of this writing, information on twenty public-interest research groups conducting operations in states other than Massachusetts is accessible via the MASSPIRG web site.

The Mission

MASSPIRG is a nonpartisan organization serving as a "watchdog" for Massachusetts citizens on issues affecting the public interest. The organization conducts multi-level campaigns in a number of different areas to defend clean air and water, provide strong safeguards for consumers, ensure a free, thriving democracy, and foster a better quality of life and a secure future for all citizens.

Words to the Wise

The staff consists largely of lawyers, scientists, and public interest professionals. For those with no professional background, administrative support jobs are available, with a large number of positions open for telemarketers. The organization frequently seeks campus organizations to reach out to students and recruit them as future leaders. MASSPIRG also offers fellowship opportunities, enabling recent college graduates to gain valuable experience in field organizing, issue advocacy, political writing, and fundraising.

What to Expect

The organization continues to exert an influence over policy issues of interest to Massachusetts citizens, and is likely to do so for some time to come.

Potent Quote

> "Our campaigns take us wherever necessary to safeguard the public interest: to the Legislature, to the courts, to corporate boardrooms, to government agencies, and the news media. With tens of thousands of members and a staff of policy specialists, MASSPIRG combines the expertise of professionals with the power of citizens in defense of clean air and water, strong safeguards for consumers, a free and vigorous democracy, and a way of living today that ensures a better quality of life for tomorrow."
>
> (From the organization's web site.)

Metropolitan Museum of Art

1000 Fifth Avenue, New York, New York 10028
212/535-7710
Fax: 212/570-3972
World Wide Web: http://www.metmuseum.org/
Contact: Human Resources

Overview

Established in 1870, the Metropolitan Museum of Art houses and promotes an art collection that emphasizes masterworks and cultural artifacts of all types and eras. It is one of the world's largest and best-known repositories and exhibitors of art, with more than five thousand years of world culture represented in its collection.

By the Numbers

Staff: 2,500.

The Metropolitan Museum engages in a wide variety of revenue-generating activities, including the operation of its Gift and Book Shop, featuring 100 museum-oriented products.

Words to the Wise

Applications for professional employment may be forwarded to the office listed above. Also of interest is the organization's internship program. The Metropolitan Museum of Art offers up to thirty-six internships in four different programs involving research, teaching, writing, and assistance with curating. Interns lead tour groups and conduct research into the collections. Internships pay a stipend that varies, based on the assignment.

What to Expect

The Metropolitan Museum of Art describes itself simply—and accurately—as "one of the largest and finest art museums in the world." This is a first-class museum facility with a considerable history, a global appeal, and a strong sense of its ongoing mission. It is likely to remain a vibrant and popular institution for many years to come.

Potent Quote

"[Our] collections include more than two million works of art—several hundred thousand of which are on view at any given time—spanning more than five thousand years of world culture, from prehistory to the present."

(From the organization's web site.)

Monterey Bay Aquarium

> *886 Cannery Road, Monterey, California 93940*
> *408/648-7902*
> *Employment Information Line: 408/648-4890*
> *World Wide Web: http://www.mbayaq.org/*
> *Contact: Human Resources*

Overview
The Monterey Bay Aquarium is one of the premier aquariums in the country devoted to entertaining and educating the public for a greater understanding of the ocean world. The Aquarium seeks to enrich quality of life in the community through its rich resources and promotion of the Monterey Bay region. Sensitive to community needs, the organization is also a worldwide leader among aquariums for its commitment to the protection of ocean resources.

By the Numbers

Staff: 350.

A recent article in *Kiplinger's Personal Finance Magazine* reported that "pay for the 20 aquarists [employees who maintain exhibits and collect specimens] ranges from $25,000 to $40,000 a year."

The Mission
The Monterey Bay Aquarium seeks to stimulate interest in and increase knowledge about the Monterey Bay in California and to promote the conservation and protection of the world's oceans through their exhibits, through public education, and scientific research. The Aquarium's mission is accomplished through innovative and creative means, with an eye toward financial self-sufficiency and with sensitivity and focus on community needs and audience interests.

Words to the Wise

There are typically thirty to forty openings a year. The best way to become a member of the Aquarium's paid staff is probably by becoming one of its volunteers. (Over eight hundred people are on the volunteer rolls at any given time.) There are nine general areas in which the Aquarium offers employment opportunities: Operations, Education, Publications, Life Sciences, Exhibits, Marketing, Merchandising, Administration, and Human Resources.

The Aquarium is dedicated to the principle of teamwork among paid staff and volunteers. By all accounts, it provides a working environment that is both creative and challenging.

What to Expect

Public interest in marine ecological issues is strong and seems likely to keep growing. The Monterey Bay Aquarium is well positioned to maintain its prominent position as one of the nation's leading aquariums.

Potent Quote

"The purpose of the Monterey Bay Aquarium is to stimulate interest, increase knowledge and promote stewardship of Monterey Bay and the world's ocean environment through innovative exhibits, public education and scientific research. This mission is to be accomplished with a high regard for quality and creativity, and with policies and programs that ensure financial self-sufficiency, a challenging and satisfying environment for employees, sensitivity to our community, and a clear focus on the needs and interests of our diverse audience."

(From the organization's web site.)

Museum of Contemporary Art

237 East Ontario, Chicago, Illinois 60611
Job Hotline: 312/397-4050
312/397-3819
Fax: 312/397-4095
World Wide Web: http://www.mcachicago.org
Contact: Human Resources Manager

Overview
Established in 1967, the Museum of Contemporary Art (MCA) in Chicago is one of the country's largest museums dedicated to contemporary visual culture. Situated since 1996 in a new building in the heart of downtown Chicago, the MCA boasts a three hundred-seat theater, a terraced garden replete with sculpture, and a magnificent view of Lake Michigan, as well as the Mayer Education Center.

By the Numbers
Staff: 65.

The Museum holds a collection of over 2,000 thought-provoking works of art and over 3,000 art books. It is noted for its special and often unusual exhibitions and art performances.

The Mission
The Museum of Contemporary Art's vision is to collect, preserve, present, and interpret contemporary art, and to broaden the audience for contemporary art through its diverse activities. The MCA focuses on international multimedia works dating from 1945 to the present day. These works include painting, sculpture, photography, video, film, and performance art.

Words to the Wise

Full- and part-time positions may be available in a number of areas. Those with art or art history backgrounds and relevant work experience may apply for jobs as curators or registrars. The Museum has both a gift store and a book store, providing openings for sales assistants, managers, and merchandise processors. Positions may also be available in marketing, accounting, and fund-raising/grant writing, as well as in the Education Outreach program, which would require some educational and program development experience. Operations experience is helpful for those who might want to work in the warehouse and buildings operations. Administrative/office support jobs may be also be available. Information about job opportunities at the MCA may be accessed by calling the Job Hotline (number above). A recent check of the organization's web site yielded specific information on openings in a variety of areas.

Students may apply for the MCA's internship program, which provides formal training, the opportunity to attend lectures, seminars, workshops, and meetings, and the possibility of full-time employment. Interns are accepted in areas as diverse as administration, development, curating, accounting, fund-raising, special events, public relations, editing, education, graphic design, and photo archives. For information about the internship program, contact Ms. Holly Ludewig, Intern Coordinator.

You can also get a foot in the door by becoming a volunteer. MCA volunteers assist in special events and hospitality, membership drives, educational programs, and general office support behind the scenes. Such experience can pave the way to a full-time job with the MCA. For information on how to become a volunteer, contact the Volunteer Coordinator.

The MCA offers diverse opportunities—both paid and unpaid—for those interested in contemporary art, as well as multi-media approaches to art presentation and preservation.

What to Expect

The Museum of Contemporary Art is one of Chicago's major cultural institutions. Its impressive new facilities—praised by *Newsweek* as "the city's best new building in years"—have gained the institution high visibility both within the city and nationally. The organization appears well positioned to pursue its distinctive mission for some time to come.

Potent Quote

"[Founded in 1967,] Chicago's newest major museum [offers] one of the nation's largest facilities devoted to the art of our time.... [The MCA provides] exhibitions of the most thought-provoking art created since 1945... [and] documents contemporary visual culture through painting, sculpture, photography, video and film, and performance.."

(From the organization's web site.)

Museum of Fine Arts, Boston

465 Huntington Avenue, Boston, Massachusetts 02115
617/267-9300 (ask for job hotline)
Fax: 617/247-6880
School of the Museum of Fine Arts employment information: 617/369-3411.
World Wide Web: http://www.mfa.org/
Contact: Human Resources

Overview

The largest institution of its kind in New England, the Museum of Fine Arts in Boston (est. 1870) is also one of the five largest art museums in the country. The museum houses a substantial collection of art objects covering numerous areas and periods of art history; it also maintains a library. The Museum offers educational opportunities in the form of lectures, films, and concerts, and operates the School of the Museum of Fine Arts.

By the Numbers

Staff: 773.

Annual revenues: $26,000,000.

The permanent collection includes over one million objects. Over one million people visit the museum each year.

The Mission

The MFA's mission is to collect, preserve, and present fine art and to support the fine arts through educational initiatives.

Words to the Wise

As of this writing, information on selected current openings within parts of the MFA can be accessed through the organization's web site. The organization also runs an active internship program.

What to Expect

The MFA is a world-class museum institution—one of the most prestigious in the country. It is committed to the ongoing fulfillment of its mission through a variety of educational and curatorial programs.

Potent Quote

"[The organization is] one of the nation's leading institutions for the exhibition and study of fine arts."

(From *Peterson's Internships 1997*.)

Museum of Science

> *Science Park, Boston, Massachusetts 02114-1099*
> *617/589-0123*
> *Fax: 617/589-0362*
> *Job Information Line: 617/589-0129*
> *Contact: Human Resources Department*
> *or Intern Program Coordinator*
> *World Wide Web: http://www.mos.org/*

Overview

Established in 1830 as the Boston Society of Natural History, Boston's Museum of Science is one of the oldest and best-known science museums in the country. Its appeal for all ages has grown steadily. In addition to its permanent and rotating exhibits, the Museum's immense resources include a Live Animal Center, a Theater of Electricity, the Mugar Omni Theater, and the Hayden Planetarium, as well as interactive areas for children and adults. Its entertaining and innovative hands-on approach to science has made it one of the leading such educational institutions in the United States.

By the Numbers

Staff: 276.

Annual revenues: $22,000,000.

Over 1.6 million people visit the Museum each year.

The Mission

The Museum of Science is committed to stimulating interest in science and technology, especially in young people, by presenting it in comprehensive and interesting ways. The Museum also seeks to promote science and technology as a way of improving everyday life and society as a whole.

Words to the Wise

The Museum of Science offers a number of career opportunities, including positions in management and part-time or full-time jobs in telemarketing. There are also staff assistant openings in various departments throughout the Museum. Instructors and teachers are frequently sought, and there is a need for overnight staff for the Camp-In Science Program. A scientific background or experience in any of these areas would serve you well. In addition, the Museum welcomes volunteers, and internships are available to qualified individuals. Interns may become involved in different areas, such as the preparation of educational materials, the training and supervisions of volunteers, the cataloging of Museum collections, assistance with writing projects, and so on. Interning provides an excellent foundation for future possible employment with the Museum.

As of this writing, information about current employment opportunities is available through the Museum's web site.

What to Expect

The Museum's press materials express a desire to remain "on the cutting edge of science education by developing innovative and interactive exhibits and programs that both entertain and educate." As the 21st century dawns, the Museum of Science appears well positioned to achieve this objective.

Potent Quote

"Over 200,000 of our visitors each year are school children and young people who come by way of school class trips; the Museum also provides important support and resources for teachers and educational administrators. To accomplish this educational mission, the staff, volunteers, overseers, and trustees of the Museum are dedicated to attracting the broadest possible spectrum of participants, and involving them in activities, exhibits, and programs that will: encourage curiosity, questioning, and exploration; inform and educate; enhance a sense of personal achievement in learning; respect individual interests, backgrounds and abilities; [and] promote life-long learning and informed and active citizenship."

(From the organization's web site.)

Museum of Television and Radio

25 West 52nd Street, New York, New York 10019
212/621-6600
World Wide Web: http://www.mtr.org/
Contact: Personnel Department

Overview

The Museum of Television and Radio (MTR) was established by William S. Paley in 1975 for the purpose of collecting and preserving radio and television history by means of exhibitions, screenings, listening series, and seminars. The Museum also provides a comprehensive educational program geared toward students at all levels. The program is designed to assist in a critical and interpretational analysis of radio and television history. A second museum in Beverly Hills, California, was opened in 1996. The Museum's total collection now includes more than 75,000 programs in a variety of areas that provide a significant representation of American art, culture, and history.

By the Numbers

Staff: 100.

The Mission

The Museum of Television and Radio is dedicated to the collection, preservation, and exhibition of radio and television programs and to making them available to the public through its New York and Beverly Hills facilities.

Words to the Wise

The MTR has an internship program that allows students to gain key experience and knowledge toward the goal of full-time employment.

Internships are offered in a number of areas, including curating, development, education, seminars, library services, public relations, publications, registration, research service, and special events.

Questions concerning full-time employment opportunities may be forwarded to the New York office.

What to Expect

The museum has expanded significantly since its inaugural year (1976), and recently launched a sister facility in California (see "Overview.") The Museum of Television and Radio appears to be well positioned for future action on behalf of its mission.

Potent Quote

"Each year the Museum, using radio and television programs from the collection, organizes major exhibitions and screenings and listening series that focus on topics of social, historical, popular, or artistic interest. Seminars feature in-person discussions with writers, producers, directors, actors, and others involved with landmark programming. In addition, the Museum's comprehensive education program welcomes special interest groups and students from the elementary to the university level and encourages them to become critical thinkers by interpreting and analyzing radio and television programs."

(From the organization's web site.)

Mystic Seaport Museum

P.O. Box 6000, Mystic, Connecticut 06335-0990
860-572-0711
Fax: 860/572-5329
World Wide Web: http://www.mysticseaport.org/
Contact: Human Resources

Overview

The Mystic Seaport Museum is a unique maritime museum covering seventeen acres in Connecticut. Numerous exhibits include three tall ships, and artifacts and paintings devoted to the seafaring life. Mystic Seaport is also committed to the preservation of ships, artifacts, and skills of previous centuries. In essence, Mystic Seaport provides "a porthole to the past."

By the Numbers

Staff: 250-400.

The Mystic Seaport Museum gains its income from a number of different sources, including gate admissions, program admissions, membership dues, food services, rentals, publishing fees, and revenue from the Museum Stores. The Museum also benefits from numerous gifts, grants, and bequests. Its endowment and investment income accounts for approximately 9 percent of its operating budget. Program expenses lay the biggest claim on Museum income (55 percent of the total operating expenses), while support in administration, maintenance, food services, and so on, account for the remaining 45 percent.

The Mission

The mission of the Mystic Seaport Museum is "to create a broad, public understanding of the relationship of America and the Sea." The museum carries out its mission through its exhibits, collections, and educational programs, and through products and publications designed to document and preserve American maritime history and stimulate the public's interest in this fascinating aspect of our country's culture. Mystic Seaport also perpetuates skills associated with the nation's maritime past and interprets certain seafaring elements of life in nineteenth-century New England.

Words to the Wise

Mystic Seaport Museum provides employment to approximately 250 full-time staff, 100 part-time staff, and close to 100 more summer employees. Employees work with exhibits and provide office and administrative support; there are also numerous opportunities in the Development and other departments. Fund-raising experience is thus your best bet for employment at the Mystic Seaport Museum, though internships and college credits often provide a doorway to permanent employment. Internships are available to college students, graduate students, career changers, people re-entering the work force, and, of course, international applicants. You may also wish to consider becoming one of the Museum's corps of more than 450 volunteers, who contribute time to fostering and maintaining Mystic Seaport's vision.

What to Expect

Right now, maintaining and developing adequate income sources is a main focus for the Museum, as it is for many in the nonprofit sector. The organization has a large and experienced development staff, which focuses expertly on this aspect of support for the organization's mission.

Potent Quote

"(V)essels are only part of the story. More than sixty buildings, authentic to the years between 1814 and 1914, are located at Mystic Seaport. Each building represents a vital element in the social and economic framework of a thriving village, from the one-room schoolhouse to the lobster shack. Exploring the entire village and the major ships would require at least a full day."

(From *Air Force Times*, August 8, 1994.)

National Association for the Advancement of Colored People

4805 Mt. Hope Drive, Baltimore, Maryland 21215-3297
410/358-8900
World Wide Web: http://www.naacp.org/
Contact: Kumar Nichani

Overview

The National Association for the Advancement of Colored People (NAACP) holds the distinction of being the oldest, largest, and best-known organization devoted to the welfare and legal rights of black citizens within the United States. Since its inception, it has worked to ensure equal access to quality education for minorities, economic empowerment, the elimination of discrimination in employment, the creation and enforcement of civil rights legislation, and minority voter registration.

The NAACP has been instrumental in the creation of the Civil Rights Acts of 1960 and 1964, the Voting Rights Act of 1965, the Fair Housing Rights Act of 1968, and the Afro-Academic, Cultural and Scientific Olympics (ACT-SO). Despite setbacks in recent years, chiefly because of internal disputes, the NAACP remains a strong and influential force in civil rights for African Americans. It describes itself—accurately enough—as the "oldest, largest, and strongest Civil Rights Organization in the United States."

By the Numbers

Staff: 120.

There are 2,200 NAACP branches in the U.S., all of which are overseen by volunteers who serve as officers. Total membership is over 500,000.

Funding is provided by membership fees and by both corporate and individual contributions.

The Mission

The NAACP works to eliminate racial prejudice and obtain equality of rights for all people of color on all political, educational, social, and economic levels. It does this through non-violent policies that use legal and moral persuasion rather than the inciting or fueling of racial hostility.

Words to the Wise

The majority of NAACP staff work in the areas of office and administrative support. Others are organizers, attorneys, lobbyists, writers, and fund raisers. On average, there are between three and five staff openings a year. Volunteers are accepted, as are interns, who usually work in the Legal Department and are given a small stipend.

What to Expect

The NAACP has long been a public and influential voice for the rights of black Americans. The organization has fought and will continue to fight to end racial stereotypes that generate prejudice and misunderstandings. The organization seeks to change attitudes, laws, and institutions in a way that will benefit all Americans and achieve a truly integrated society. This attitude has been regarded as too passive by some black Americans, and the NAACP has received criticism both for its approach and for perceptions of divisions and in-fighting among its leadership. However, the group now seems to be on the road to regaining much of its former prestige and stature. The NAACP will probably continue to play an important role in American life and culture for many years to come.

Potent Quote

"On the 100th anniversary of Abraham Lincoln's birthday, sixty prominent black and white citizens issued 'The Call' for a national conference in New York City to renew 'the struggle for civil and political liberty.' A distinguished group of black leaders added [its] voice to the movement. Principal among these was W.E.B. DuBois, who was to serve as the sage of black professionals to form the Niagara Movement, which drew up an agenda for aggressive action not unlike the group he now joined. Also involved was Ida Wells-Barnett, a young journalist whose eloquent editorials focused national attention on the epidemic of lynchings. Participants at the conference agreed to work together toward the abolition of forced segregation, the promotion of equal education and civil rights under the protection of law, and an end to race violence. In 1911, that organization was incorporated as the National Association for the Advancement of Colored People—the NAACP."

(From the organization's web site.)

National Audubon Society

> *700 Broadway, New York, New York 10003*
> *212/979-3000*
> *World Wide Web: http://www.Audubon.org/*
> *Contact: Patricia Ryan, Human Resources*

Overview

The National Audubon Society is a well-known organization devoted to conservation of the environment and its wildlife. Through research, educational programs, lobbying, and litigation, the Society strives to protect the planet and seek global solutions for problems involving the interaction of the human animal with earth's creatures and resources. Stressing environmental education for children, the Society produces numerous television and classroom programs and also publishes a number of magazines and newsletters. It also works with local chapters to enlist membership and to create and maintain wildlife sanctuaries all over the country. The organization monitors environmental legislation at all levels of government and works to ensure the enforcement of conservation laws. It is one of the most active and influential forces in environmental protection today.

By the Numbers

Staff: 350 full-time; 30 part-time.

Budget: $44,500,000.

Contributions are received directly from individuals and foundations, as well as through direct mail campaigns and telephone solicitations. Program services—education and publishing—receive 65 percent of the Society's income; the remainder goes to fund-raising and administrative costs.

The Mission

The National Audubon Society seeks to benefit humanity and the planet by working to conserve and restore natural ecosystems. The organization's primary focus is on birds and other wildlife, but it also has turned its attention to issues of pollution, land use, and energy resources.

Words to the Wise

The staff includes managers, fund raisers, researchers, lobbyists, accountants, and office support staff. There are about ten staff openings a year; check the newspaper and the listings of other environmental organizations. There are also openings for about thirty summer employees. Interns in the areas of environmental policy and conservation science are accepted for a stay of three months and provided with housing and a stipend.

What to Expect

Guided by the principle that the preservation of the natural heritage is everyone's responsibility, the Audubon Society has fought and won many battles over the years, resulting in significant progress in the area of environmental policy. Through educational and outreach programs, the Society has also helped build public awareness of the role all of us can play in conservation efforts. The Society recently prepared a long-term strategic plan for the coming century that calls for a greater focus on the conservation of bird and other wildlife, along with their habitats. They plan to broaden their educational programs to promote public understanding of the link between a sound ecology and human survival, and to invest heavily in the existing grassroots network for environmental advocacy. In these ways they hope to create a "culture of conservation" throughout the country and the world.

Potent Quote

"Major efforts for the 1990s include protecting ancient forests in the Pacific Northwest, preventing oil drilling in the Arctic National Wildlife Refuge, preserving wetlands, and reauthorizing the Endangered Species Act."

(From the organization's web site.)

National Baseball Hall of Fame

P.O. Box 590, 25 Main Street, Cooperstown, New York 13326
607/547-7200
Fax: 607/547-2044
World Wide Web: http://www.baseballhalloffame.org
Contact: Personnel Office

Overview

The National Baseball Hall of Fame is probably one of the most famous museums in the country, if not the world, thanks to its relentless devotion to America's favorite pastime. It was established in 1935 in Cooperstown, New York—the legendary birthplace of baseball—and dedicated in June 1939, on the hundredth anniversary of the game's beginnings. Since then it has grown both in size and in reputation, becoming a kind of Mecca for baseball fans and historians. With improved computer technology and its expansion onto the World Wide Web, the Hall of Fame now seeks to become a "virtual museum," making its vast databases on the history of baseball available to all on-line. This will not, however, diminish the popularity of its complex of buildings in Cooperstown, including the Hall of Fame Gallery, the National Baseball Library, and the Fetzer-Yawkey Building. Through its efforts on behalf of the game, the National Baseball Hall of Fame has itself become an American institution.

By the Numbers

The Museum oversees a number of revenue-generating activities. Annual paid attendance at the museum "regularly approaches 350,000." The organization completed an $8 million expansion of its library in 1994. The Hall of Fame's web site—a favorite for many Internet-savvy baseball fans—now features over two hundred pages.

The Mission
The National Baseball Hall of Fame and Museum is an educational institution dedicated to the game and the history of baseball. It seeks by a variety of means to foster appreciation for the game's impact on American culture. These means include collecting and exhibiting historical artifacts and other materials, providing educational programs, and honoring those who have made significant contributions to the game by enshrining them in the Hall of Fame.

Words to the Wise
Questions concerning employment openings may be forwarded to the Cooperstown office.

What to Expect
The National Baseball Hall of Fame remains one of the most popular sports institutions in the country. It continues to open new exhibits, and visitor attendance appears to be growing. The Hall of Fame has recently expanded its audience by going online, making its educational programs and its library and archival files available worldwide. There is no question that it will continue to play a major role in the growth and development of the sport of baseball.

Potent Quote

"The biggest day of the year, of course, is Hall of Fame Day, when the newly elected members are inducted. Many league executives, club officials, former players and coaches and previously-inducted Hall of Famers participate in the emotion-packed program, witnessed by thousands of baseball fans from all over the United States and Canada. The following day, two major league teams clash in the annual Hall of Fame Game at Doubleday Field. The ball field, just a block from the Museum, is located on the former Elihu Phinney cow pasture where baseball was once believed to have been played more than a century ago by Doubleday and his friends. The Village Board of Trustees transformed the erstwhile pasture into a ballpark of major league specifications in 1939, and it now seats approximately 10,000 fans."

(From the organization's web site.)

National Organization for Women

> *100 16th Street NW*
> *Washington, D.C. 20036*
> *202/331-0066*
> *Fax: 202/785-8576*
> *World Wide Web: http://www.now.org/*
> *Contact: Cindy Hanford*

Overview

Founded in 1966, the National Organization for Women (NOW) is the largest group of feminist activists in America.

By the Numbers

The group has approximately 250,000 members and 600 chapters in all 50 states and in Washington, D.C.

The Mission

NOW members use "both traditional and nontraditional means" to make equality for women a reality. A historical commitment to issues that are not necessarily embraced by the political mainstream continues to exert a powerful influence over the organization's agenda. In 1967, for instance, NOW was the first national group to "call for the legalization of abortion and the repeal of all abortion laws." In recent years, NOW has embraced a variety of controversial causes as part of its campaign to win equality for women.

Words to the Wise

As of this writing, the group's web site features specific information on particular job openings. There is an internship program. Voluntarism plays an important role in the group's education, coaching, and advocacy activities.

What to Expect

NOW continues to live up to its reputation for aggressive action in pursuit of its goals, advocating and lobbying on a number of fronts. A major shift in organizational emphasis in recent years has been the decision to focus "less on trying to influence men in power and more on electing feminists to replace them." This goal is likely to remain a prominent one in the years to come, and to resonate positively with NOW's committed body of members. NOW's continued focus on issues like abortion and gay rights will also guarantee the group its share of vocal critics.

Potent Quote

"NOW is dedicated to making legal, political, social, and economic change in our society in order to achieve our goal, which is to eliminate sexism and end all oppression."

(From the organization's web site.)

National Rifle Association

> *11250 Waples Mill Road Fairfax VA 22030*
> *703/267-1110*
> *World Wide Web: http://www.nra.org/*
> *Contact: Human Resources Department*

Overview

The National Rifle Association (NRA) is the nation's most prominent advocacy group on behalf of the shooting sports. It is active in a wide variety of educational and lobbying activities, including a broad array of gun safety and community service programs.

Founded in 1871, the group is the oldest sportsman's association in the United States. The NRA's membership is a powerful force in national politics; members are highly motivated to preserve the rights of sports shooters and promote the safe and responsible use of firearms.

By the Numbers

Staff: Over 300.

Budget: Approximately $80 million.

The group boasts 2.6 million members.

The Mission

The NRA is dedicated to the promotion of responsible sport-shooting activities and to the defense of Constitutionally specified rights relating to firearms.

Words to the Wise

Questions concerning employment openings may be forwarded to the Fairfax office.

What to Expect

With more than sixty-five million owners of firearms in the U.S., the potential for growth and continued promotion of the NRA's mission is significant. Like a number of other organizations included in this book, the NRA's mission has controversial elements likely to evoke criticism and opposition from some corners of society.

One of the group's most interesting current initiatives is Crime-Strike, which promotes "Keep Killers in Prison" and "Silent No More" programs on behalf of the victims and survivors of violent crime.

Potent Quote

"Service to our membership requires the talents and expertise of a dedicated staff. Over three hundred highly professional and extremely motivated men and women work every day in our Fairfax, Virginia, NRA headquarters. In addition, the NRA membership is served by a staff of field representatives located across the nation."

(From the organization's web site.)

National Urban League, Inc.

> *120 Wall Street, 8th floor, New York NY 10005*
> *212/310-9000*
> *World Wide Web: http://www.nul.org/*
> *Contact: Dorothy Millines, Recruitment Specialist*

Overview

The National Urban League (NUL) seeks to improve the quality of life and to achieve social and economic parity for African Americans. Its tireless work has included such projects as the National Education Initiative, the Comprehensive Youth Development Program, the AIDS Initiative, Stop the Violence Clearinghouse, the Seniors in Community Service Program, and the Black Executive Exchange Program (BEEP). The League has also concentrated on such issues as adolescent pregnancy and parenting and on environmental employment, especially for seniors. With its community-based approach to fostering self-sufficiency and racial inclusion and a constituency of more than two million, the NUL is considered to be one of the top social service and civil rights organizations in the U.S.

By the Numbers

Staff: 200

Budget: $27,000,000.

Funding is received from a combination of corporate and labor donations, foundation and government grants, and individual contributions.

The Mission

The National Urban League seeks to bring about social and economic equality for African Americans through human services, community organizing, public education, advocacy efforts, training and technical assistance, and similar bridge-building approaches. Attainment of these goals, the League hopes, will gradually narrow the gaps between African Americans and other Americans in such areas as educational opportunities, employment parity, and economic status.

Words to the Wise

The organization is headquartered in New York City, maintains a research department in Washington, D.C., and has 114 affiliates in 34 states. The staff consists primarily of social workers, economists, administrators, and office support personnel. Part-time employees are hired on a consultant basis. Summer jobs and internships (with stipend) are available, but the League's large corps of volunteers (30,000 nation-wide), probably provides the best opportunity for access, as most jobs are advertised internally. Its web site also lists job search possibilities.

What to Expect

Approximately 114 Urban League affiliates serve more than two million African Americans, operating programs in education, job training and placement, crime prevention, housing, and Business Development. With its large constituency and wide range of services, the NUL continues to play a major role in supporting self-sufficiency and self-respect among the African American community.

Potent Quote

"The National Urban League, under the new leadership of Hugh B. Price, has sought to emphasize greater reliance on the unique resources and strengths of the African-American community to find solutions to its own problems. To accomplish this, the League's approach has been to utilize fully the tools of advocacy, research, program service and systems change. The result has been an organization with strong roots in the community, focused on the social and educational development of youth, economic self-sufficiency, and racial inclusion."

(From the organization's web site.)

National Wildlife Federation

8925 Leesburg Pike, Vienna, Virginia 22184-0001
703/790-4100
Job hotline: 703/790-4522
World Wide Web: http://www.nwf.org/nwf/
Contact: Human Resources Department
For internships, contact Nancy Hwa, Administrative Coordinator

Overview

The National Wildlife Federation (NWF) is one of the largest environmental protection organizations in the world, with nearly five million
members and supporters covering a wide range of demographic groups.
The organization achieves its goals in wildlife and environmental conservation through such methods as lobbying, public education, research,
and litigation, as well as through the sale of publications and merchandise. The NWF has been instrumental in the passage of such initiatives
as the Endangered Species Act, Range-Land Reform, the preservation of
ancient forests, and the Great Lakes Initiative. Its primary focus, however, is on education, whether based in the community, in the outdoors,
or in the classroom. Through the publication of *Ranger Rick* magazine,
the NWF teaches children about nature and its conservancy and encourages exploration of the environment. The group also trains teachers in
various curricula, distributes educational materials to classrooms nationwide, and keeps its members informed about pending environmental
legislation.

By the Numbers

Staff: 650.

Budget: $90,000,000.

The NWF is the largest member-supported conservation group in the
U.S., with a national network of ten field offices and forty-five affiliated

organizations. Support is largely received through member fees, youth memberships, and contributions from individuals, organizations, businesses, and government. An additional percentage of the organization's funding is derived from the sale of nature education materials, including a catalog of gifts, cards, etc. Programs and services receive 62 percent of income, while 28 percent goes towards fund-raising expenses. The remainder is applied to administrative and other costs.

The Mission

The National Wildlife Federation seeks to conserve wildlife and the natural resources through education, inspiration, and assistance to people and organizations from diverse cultures. Its philosophy is that responsible and effective education in conservation promotes a peaceful and life-sustaining future for all.

Words to the Wise

The Federation has about twenty entry-level openings a year for writers/editors, attorneys, issue experts, lobbyists, researchers, organizers, fund raisers, and administrative and support staff. It also accepts a limited number of part-time employees and volunteers, and interns, both paid and unpaid, for periods of up to 6 months. Positions are posted internally for three days before being opened to outside candidates by means of newspaper advertisements. As of this writing, the organization's web site also details specific job vacancies. Timing appears to play a key role in many job vacancies; applicants may wish to monitor the NWF web page closely and act quickly when an opening presents itself.

What to Expect

Although the organization is active on a number of environmental fronts, its continuing focus is on activism, advocacy, and litigation. Because of its effectiveness in addressing issues of deep concern to many Americans, the NWF is likely to retain a leadership position in future national debates on the environment.

Potent Quote

"At the National Wildlife Federation, positions are posted for internal candidates for a minimum of three days. After a position has cleared internal job posting, it is open to outside candidates until filled, unless a closing date has been specified. Resumes are only accepted for posted positions."

(Excerpt from the organization's "Job Opportunities" web page. Timing appears to play a key role in many job vacancies; applicants may wish to monitor this page closely and act quickly.)

The Nature Conservancy

1815 North Lynn Street, Arlington, Virginia 22209
703/247-3721 (Job hotline)
World Wide Web: http://www.tnc.org/
Contact: Personnel and Administration

Overview

The Nature Conservancy is an international organization devoted to the preservation of the natural environment. Its constituency includes corporations, private business, and concerned individuals. In addition to pursuing its own initiatives, the Conservancy works closely with other environmental organizations and with certain universities on research and common goals. It has been involved in innumerable initiatives to protect key natural sites in many states, in hundreds of land/species protection projects, and in debt-for-nature swaps in various countries. The organization is also known for its efforts in the Connecticut River Protection Campaign and the Delaware Bay and Basin Campaign. The Conservancy often purchases and donates land to groups dedicated to preserving wildlife habitats and ecosystems. It also operates the largest private system of nature sanctuaries in the world, with more than 1,500 preserves in the U.S. alone. The Conservancy's successful work has earned it the title of "Nature's real estate agent."

By the Numbers

Staff: 831.

Budget: $81,700,000.

Funding is derived primarily from individual and corporate contributions, foundation grants, and direct mail solicitations. Of the total, 60 percent goes into programs and services, 15 percent goes into fundraising and administration, and the remainder is invested.

The Mission

The Nature Conservancy works to protect the lands, waters, and natural resources necessary to sustain plant and animal life on earth, and by so doing to ensure the biological preservation of diverse natural communities throughout the world.

Words to the Wise

The Conservancy may have up to four hundred openings a year for fund raisers, membership administrators, and support staff. It also employs life scientists, attorneys, lobbyists, and writer/editors. Other opportunities sometimes arise in the areas of legal and government relations, communications, science and stewardship, information systems, accounting, and finance. Jobs are advertised internally, through newspaper ads, and via the publications *Environmental Opportunities* and *Job Seeker*. Job opportunities may also be accessed through the organization's Job Hot Line.

What to Expect

The Nature Conservancy's innovative, active, and effective approach to environmental preservation is likely to play an important role in the nature sanctuary movement for many years to come. This is an excellent target organization for environmentally minded job seekers.

Potent Quote

> "The Conservancy works only with willing sellers and donors. We protect land through gifts, exchanges, conservation easements, management agreements, purchases from the Conservancy's revolving Land Preservation Fund, debt-for-nature swaps, and management partnerships. The Conservancy manages the resulting preserves with the most sophisticated ecological techniques available."

> (From the organization's web site.)

The Network, Inc.

300 Brickstone Square, Suite 900, Boston, Massachusetts 01810
508/470-1080
Contact: Personnel Director

Overview

The Network, Inc. works to improve public education through training, technical assistance, and human services. It also conducts education-related research, puts out a number of newsletters and other publications, and lobbies on behalf of public education. The group has been instrumental in the development of the National Center for Improving Science Education, the Center for Effective Communications, the Ford Academy of Manufacturing Sciences, and the Regional Educational Laboratory, serving New York, New England, Puerto Rico, and the U.S. Virgin Islands.

By the Numbers

Staff: 110.

Budget: $5,000,000.

Funding comes primarily from federal grants and contracts, with additional income derived from foundations and direct client support.

The Mission

The Network, Inc. seeks to foster organizational change in local schools and other educational organizations through research, resources, and problem-solving. Its long-term vision is for equity and quality in educational systems nationwide.

Words to the Wise

The majority of staff members are either issue experts or providers of training and/or technical assistance. The Network also has a small core of researchers, plus about five writers/editors and three fund raisers. Otherwise, entry-level positions may be found in the general office support area. There are a limited number of part-time and summer employees, and only two internships a year. Jobs are advertised in newspapers, professional publications, and through sister organizations. Job postings may also be found at the Division of Employment Security.

What to Expect

The Network, Inc. is an established research and advocacy group that offers competitive pay rates, with excellent starting salaries. This tends to attract employees who welcome challenge and the opportunity for achievement. The average Network work week can apparently be rather long. Applicants should probably be prepared for an intense commitment to their work and to Network's cause.

Potent Quote

"The Network, Inc. was founded in 1969 to link innovative schools in Massachusetts with one another and has developed into a highly regarded research and development organization that conducts a wide array of services designed to enhance learning. These include evaluation, research, product development, dissemination, training, and technical assistance conducted throughout the U.S. as well as internationally. Our staff is augmented by scores of highly respected national and international consultants. Throughout our history, we have collaborated with and provided services for state and federal agencies, colleges and universities, schools, research and development laboratories and centers, and private businesses, helping them to define problems, find solutions, and use what they learned to improve education and enhance learning in children and adults."

(From *Who We Are*, organization's mission statement.)

New England Aquarium

> *177 Milk Street, Boston, Massachusetts 02110*
> *617/973-5200*
> *617/973-0289 (Job hotline)*
> *Fax: 617/720-5098*
> *World wide web: http://www.neaq.org/*
> *Contact: Director, Human Resources*

Overview

Since 1969, exhibits, education, and research programs have made the New England Aquarium a world leader in the preservation and conservation of our water environment.. Every year more than a million visitors come to see the Aquarium's superb exhibitions of aquatic life and habitats, featuring an amazing diversity of marine life. Educational and research programs focus on critical New England species, habitats, and issues. In this and other ways the Aquarium provides an internationally respected and effective voice for aquatic conservation.

By the Numbers

Staff: 150-200.

Annual revenues: $15,000,000.

The organization recently projected an annual visitor total of 1.6 million.

The Mission

The New England Aquarium seeks to increase public awareness and understanding of marine life, to conserve and protect the aquatic world, and to lead the way in the sustainable use of water-based resources.

Words to the Wise

The New England Aquarium values talent and dedication in all its employees, from clerks and visitor's assistants to supervisors and managers. The Aquarium offers a variety of job openings in areas as diverse as finance, development, purchasing, conservation, animal husbandry, education, operations, sales, food services, and visitor services. Expertise in setting up special programs and exhibits would be a plus, as would solid office experience. As of this writing, descriptions of openings can be found at the organization's web site.

What to Expect

The New England Aquarium is currently in the process of a major expansion at its site on the Boston waterfront, increasing both the size of its facility and the scope of its programs. This long-range project, known as Aquarium 2000, stresses informal science education, conservation, and research as the Aquarium responds to increasing environmental risks and problems. Their plans are ambitious and seem likely set a new standard for waterfront activities around the world. They will also create numerous new job opportunities for individuals possessing the skills, education, experience, and dedication to meet the conservation challenges of the twenty-first century.

Potent Quote

"[Our] ambitious plans will create a multitude of challenges, as well as opportunities for qualified individuals who will bring a wide range of skills, education, and experience to fill numerous positions… The New England Aquarium values the talent and dedication of its staff and provides a competitive salary and a comprehensive benefits package."

(From the organization's Human Resources materials.)

Ohio Citizen Action

> *402 Terminal Tower, 50 Public Square, Cleveland, OH 44113*
> *216/861-5200*
> *Contact: Personnel Department*

Overview

Using environmental and consumer issues as a focal point, Ohio Citizen Action fosters the involvement of ordinary citizens in the democratic process by a combination of research, lobbying, public education, training and technical assistance, community organizing, publications, litigation, and direct action. Ohio Citizen Action has supported the Great Lakes Water Quality Initiative, the Federal Pollution Prevention Bill, insurance reform, and issues affecting energy and utility policy.

By the Numbers

Staff: 172.

Budget: $4,000,000.

Income for Ohio Citizen Action is derived primarily from canvassing and telephone solicitations, along with foundation donations and individual contributions. With a membership base of 425,000 people, the organization recruits new members by door-to-door canvassing.

The Mission

The goal of Ohio Citizen Action is to bring about democratic change by promoting and assisting in citizen action.

Words to the Wise

Most staff members are canvassers, supported by organizers and office staff, one writer/editor, one lobbyist, one press aide, and one foundation fund raiser. There are usually only two or three staff openings a year, along with occasional openings for part-time and summer employees. Interns are accepted for periods of three to six months. Jobs are advertised in newspapers and magazines and posted at related organizations.

What to Expect

Hours are likely to be long and pay comparatively low for staff members. Consider exploring employment possibilities with this established, experienced, and effective advocacy group because you care about the issues it is working on—not because you see the chance for significant financial remuneration.

Potent Quote

"Ohio Citizen Action can call on the financial support of 425,000 members developed by door-to-door canvassing campaigns that highlight consumer and environmental issues. Its high-circulation publications include *Citizen Action* and *Toxic Watch*."

(Summary, BBP Services Newsletter, December, 1997.)

Outward Bound

Route 9D , R2 Box 280, Garrison, New York 10524-9757
1-800/243-8520 or 914/424-4000
World Wide Web: http://www.outwardbound.org/
Contact: "Call for packet of positions available at individual schools."

Overview

Outward Bound is a renowned and highly respected program that uses wilderness expeditions to provide intensive character training to enrollees. The focus is especially on teamwork and survival skills.

Students who enroll in Outward Bound's courses range from young people to corporate executives, all seeking to learn how to take risks and endure in a challenging environment. Outward Bound's lessons can later be applied to non-wilderness situations—the "real world" of job layoffs, increased workloads, and prolonged stress and pressure in the family or the workplace.

Most of the organization's programs are courses in wilderness adventures, although it also provides classroom-oriented courses in professional development, and some urban and educational programs. With more than fifty schools and centers on five continents, Outward Bound has won widespread recognition for its success at helping participants improve their self-confidence, social responsiveness, and personal physical fitness.

Overview

Staff: 200 full-time employees; 1,800 seasonal employees.

Budget: $38,000,000.

Outward Bound is funded by membership fees and supplemented by government grants, endowments, and charitable gifts.

The Mission

Outward Bound conducts safe, adventure-based programs designed to instill respect for oneself and for others, as well as care and consideration for the environment. It was founded by Kurt Hahn, a German refugee in Britain during World War II, with the express mission of helping British merchant seamen survive the rigors of the high seas in case their vessels were torpedoed by German submarines. The program was brought to the United States in 1962 by Joshua Miner, a Boston-based educator.

In peacetime, Outward Bound has evolved into a survival training program for any person willing to apply him- or herself to an intense, difficult, and exacting daily regimen in the wilderness. The program's two best-known courses are "the ropes course" and "the Wall," which have become metaphors for overcoming challenges that at first seem insurmountable. The Outward Bound philosophy is built upon the belief that learning and understanding become possible when challenging experiences force people to acquire new skills, make choices, take responsible action, and work with others. By providing this catalyst for change and personal growth, Outward Bound lives up to its catalog slogan, "The adventure lasts a lifetime."

Words to the Wise

Each Outward Bound school is responsible for hiring its own teaching staff, and the primary need appears to be for qualified instructors. Application should be made directly to the Outward Bound school of your choice, with the understanding that most field employment opportunities are seasonal. Guidelines for requirements and qualifications are very strict; make sure you examine them thoroughly before submitting an application. Those who seek relevant experience with an eye toward future employment may become interns, at a stipend of $50 a week. Internships are conducted during the summer for a duration of eight weeks. Interns receive field training, assist instructors on expeditions, and perform a variety of chores. About 70 percent of interns are later hired for instructors' positions.

Applicants must have certification in CPR, advanced first aid, and lifeguard training. Some schools may also be seeking rock-climbing specialists. The Outward Bound web site provides a good resource for information on job openings and requirements.

What to Expect

Outward Bound has been criticized by some for a supposedly unchanging approach, and for emphasizing personal growth in its programs over practical wilderness survival skills. Its annual enrollment has dropped from over 13,000 members in 1986 to about 9,000 in 1997. The organization has also picked up some competition along the way. One competitor, the National Outdoor Leadership School based in Lander, Wyoming, has emphasized wilderness education and survival skills. All in all, Outward Bound has suffered some setbacks in recent years. At the same time, the modern phenomena of downsizing, increased workloads, and job layoffs have brought about increased enrollment by corporate executives and managers, leading numerous chapters of the organization to expand programs in professional development. This increased emphasis on personal growth remains a primary focus for Outward Bound.

The organization plans to revamp its education programs in an effort to reach teenagers with a learn-by-doing approach, and to tailor expeditions as ongoing educational experiences.

If you love the outdoors, possess the technical skills for teaching wilderness survival, relate well to others, and can work with people from all kinds of social, racial, and economic backgrounds, this is the place for you. Outward Bound provides a rigorous, challenging environment for clientele and instructors alike.

Be aware that becoming an instructor does not involve simply "knowing the ropes." You must also have the appropriate "people skills." You will be subjected to a thorough screening process that will assess your maturity, judgment, and experience working with people in stressful situations. Basic knowledge of survival skills will not suffice; your expertise must be considerably greater than that of the average hiker or camper. You must also demonstrate competence in teaching, counseling, and guiding. Applicants should expect an intensive screening and training process.

Potent Quote

"Outward Bound courses are designed to help people develop confidence, compassion, an appreciation for selfless service to others, and a lasting relationship with the natural environment. We are *not* a survival school. We do offer, however, a rugged adventure in the wilderness during which you will receive unparalleled training in wilderness skills. Ours is a unique, rigorous curriculum in which you will learn by doing, and put your learning to the test daily."

(From the organization's web site.)

People for the Ethical Treatment of Animals

501 Front Street, Norfolk, Virginia 23510
757/622-PETA (7382)
Fax: 757/628-0738
World Wide Web: http://www.peta-online.org/
Contact: Jennifer Vines, Personnel Director

Overview

With over 400,000 members, from celebrities to anonymous contributors, People for the Ethical Treatment of Animals (PETA, est. 1980) is the largest and one of the best-known organizations dedicated to animal rights. It has achieved both acclaim and criticism for its actions in such endeavors as persuading major companies to stop testing products on animals and convincing people to stop wearing fur or to use products that contain animal ingredients. PETA uses a variety of methods to achieve its goals, including organizing educational programs to inform the public on animal abuse and promote alternative, respectful ways to treat animals; investigating cruelty cases; and seeking the enforcement of laws and regulations protecting animals. They have also put together special events that draw attention to their cause through the direct support and involvement of celebrities. This has made PETA the most highly-publicized group devoted to the concerns of animals.

By the Numbers

Budget: $10,000,000.

Funding for PETA is provided primarily by individual contributions, supplemented by direct mail campaigns, foundations, and sales from merchandise. Programs and services receive 79 percent of its funding; the remainder goes toward fund-raising and administration.

The Mission

PETA is an advocate for the rights of nonhuman animals. It works to end human exploitation of other species. Educational programs, cruelty investigations, rescue operations, advocacy, special events, and direct action are all activities it has undertaken. PETA endorses a vegan-based lifestyle free of cruelty to animals; it seeks to effect positive changes in the ways humans regard and interact with other species. The guiding principle for the organization is: "Animals are not ours to eat, wear, experiment on, or use for entertainment."

Words to the Wise

PETA has about fifteen staff openings a year in a variety of positions, from general office support to writers and editors, issue experts, and organizers. It accepts up to ten interns for periods of two to four weeks and also hires fifteen additional staff every summer. Volunteers are welcome to assist in a variety of activities, from clerical work to outreach programs. Jobs are advertised in the Washington Post and occasionally in the Non-Profit Times, and, of course, internally. As of this writing, job opportunities are also listed on their web site.

What to Expect

PETA is not, and is not soon likely to be, a universally popular organization. The simple fact that an overwhelming majority of Americans are meat eaters means that the lifestyles of most of our readers probably conflict directly with PETA's mission statement.

Many people who uphold the right of other species to coexist peacefully with humans would find the group's work highly satisfying. PETA has been criticized for some of its methods, however, and its media coverage has not always been positive. Many consider the organization an extremist one that has occasionally gone too far in its campaigns to publicize and curtail cruelty to animals. Before you explore employment opportunities here, you should probably evaluate PETA's history and projects closely to make sure you and the organization are compatible.

Potent Quote

"PETA focuses its attention on the four areas in which the largest numbers of animals suffer the most intensely for the longest period of time: on factory farms, in laboratories, in the fur trade, and in the entertainment industry. We also work on a variety of other issues, including the cruel killing of beavers, birds and other 'pests,' and the abuse of backyard dogs. PETA works through public education, cruelty investigations, research, animal rescue, legislation, special events, celebrity involvement, and direct action."

(From the organization's mission statement.)

Planned Parenthood Federation of America, Inc.

810 Seventh Avenue, New York, New York 10019
212/541-7800
World Wide Web: http://www.ppfa.org/ppfa/
Contact: Marlene Zeilin

Overview

The nation's largest and oldest family planning agency, Planned Parenthood of America uses human services, lobbying, litigation, public education, community organizing, and research to achieve its goal of free choice in family planning. PPFA has played a major (and often controversial) role in national debate over reproductive rights issues, and is active on the state level as an advocate for comprehensive reproductive health and education services. It has also worked to establish standards and protocols in medicine, and to provide information, financial assistance, and technical support to its 144 affiliates and to health projects throughout the world. The organization's staff and extensive network of volunteers provide family planning services to more then five million Americans each year.

By the Numbers

Staff: 235.

Budget: $40,000,000.

PPFA is funded through a variety of sources, including income from clinics and donor gifts. Over 500,000 donors provide nearly 24 percent of PPFA's support. The organization receives additional support from foundations, corporations, and direct mail solicitations. Of the total, 66 percent goes to patient services; the rest is divided among fund-raising activities, community and educational services, management costs, and investments.

The Mission

Planned Parenthood Federation of America is dedicated to the guiding principle of free choice in having children and to the ideal of becoming a parent by choice rather than chance. The organization believes that each individual has the right to make a decision about whether and when to bring a child into the world, and that this decision should be a private one. Such self-determination, Planned Parenthood argues, will help to enhance the quality of life for all, ensuring strong family relationships as well as population stability.

PPFA works to provide comprehensive reproductive and health care services in an environment that preserves the rights of all individuals; to ensure access to their services through legal advocacy measures; to educate the public to understand human sexuality and its societal and individual implications; and to promote scientific and technological research relating to reproductive health care and its effect on society.

Words to the Wise

Planned Parenthood's nine hundred locations nationwide provide a comprehensive range of educational and health care services to both women and men. Any of these are likely to have occasional administrative and health care openings, as is the national office in New York. PPFA relies on efficient administrative support, so office experience is a plus. Some of the more specialized and limited positions include campaign managers, attorneys, writers/editors, lobbyists, organizers, fund raisers, and researchers. However, the greatest need is usually for clinical assistance (physicians, nurses) and office support.

Because Planned Parenthood serves people from all socioeconomic and racial backgrounds, diverse language skills and a demonstrated ability to work in specific cultural settings could work in your favor. Jobs are advertised through job bulletins and support staff listings, and, as of this writing, are also listed on the PPFA web site.

What to Expect

Some nonprofits pursue missions that virtually everyone can support, or at least accept. Planned Parenthood is not one of them. Its involvement in complex and often bitterly disputed questions relating to reproductive education and care have resulted in a legacy of conflict and controversy that can be traced to the organization's very earliest days. There is no reason to believe that this state of affairs will change in years to come.

If you believe in the rights of people to make their own decisions regarding reproduction, then you could well find working for PPFA to be a highly satisfying experience. You should, however, be aware that both the organization and its mission have their detractors.

Potent Quote

"Planned Parenthood, the nation's oldest and largest reproductive health care agency, with 900 locations nationwide, provides a comprehensive range of educational and health care services to five million people each year. We are concerned with the health and well-being of women and men, the family, and the community. Put your skills to work for a cause you believe in. By making Planned Parenthood your career choice, you make reproductive choice a reality for others. Your professional expertise, your language skills, and your cultural sensitivity are all needed in order for us to effectively serve our diverse communities."

(From the organization's "Job Listings" web page.)

The Population Council

1 Dag Hammarskjold Plaza, New York, New York 10017
212/339-0500
Fax: 212-755-6052
World Wide Web: http://www.popcouncil.org/
Contact: Benjamin Bilbao

Overview

The Population Council (PC), a non-governmental research organization established in 1952, is a vigorous advocate for the use of contraception in controlling the growth of the world's population, especially in developing countries. It accomplishes its goals through research and development programs, direct action, and the dissemination of information on population issues. It also funds fellowships for students pursuing population-related studies. PC covers numerous areas of population control, including reproductive physiology and health, family planning, contraception, and women's issues.

By the Numbers

Staff: 360.

Budget: $49,000,000.

PC's funding is derived from governments and non-government organizations, as well as from foundations, multilateral organizations, corporations, and individual contributions.

The Mission

The Population Council works to promote responsible population control in developing countries through educational and research programs in health and the social sciences. The Council also seeks to develop and improve contraceptive technology through biomedical research, and to provide technical assistance and advice to international governments and agencies. Its work to improve the reproductive health and overall well-being of people worldwide also plays a role in attaining an equitable and sustainable balance between people and resources that benefits both present and future generations.

Words to the Wise

PC's research and programs are divided into three areas: the Center for Biomedical research, the Policy Research Division, and the International Programs Division. In addition to the New York headquarters, the Council maintains four regional and fifteen overseas offices. Its staff is international, with 360 men and women from more than 60 countries around the world. Thus, employment opportunities can be quite competitive. If you have an advanced degree and/or a strong background in population control, you have a better chance of a position. As of this writing, the Council's web site lists many job possibilities, including positions in research, development, management, and administrative support. Fellowships are also offered to qualified individuals; through such awards the Council has helped to advance the careers of over two thousand social and biomedical scientists.

What to Expect

Population Council—insulated, to a degree, from regional political concerns by its strong international focus—is well positioned to continue the pursuit of its mission.

Potent Quote

"About 360 women and men from more than 60 countries work for the Council, about a third of whom hold advanced degrees. Roughly 40 percent are based in developing countries. Council staff collaborate with developing-country colleagues to conduct research and programs in some 50 countries."

(From *General Information about the Council.*)

Project Now Community Action Agency

> *418 19th Street, PO Box 3970, Rock Island, Illinois 61201*
> *309/793-6391*
> *Contact: Vincent G. Thomas, Executive Director*

Overview

Project Now Community Action Agency combats poverty by providing services, training, assistance, and educational materials to a wide constituency of disadvantaged persons. Its work includes finding housing for the homeless and rehabilitating vacant housing units. It assists those with low incomes to find decent, affordable homes, set up entrepreneurial businesses, and secure bank loans. In addition to its Rock Island headquarters, PNCAA maintains branch offices in Moline and East Moline, Kewanee, and Aledo, Illinois.

By the Numbers

Staff: 150.

Budget: $4,800,000.

Government funding makes up 75 percent of PNCAA's income. Foundations donate 15 percent , and the remainder comes from fundraising and individual contributions.

The Mission

PNCAA's goal is to fight poverty by working at the national, state, and local levels to identify, organize, and make full use of all available resources, both human and material.

Words to the Wise

There are usually only a few staff openings a year. The greatest need is for caseworkers. Part-time and summer employees are part of the employment mix. Interns receive a small stipend and assist in special projects and community organizing. Jobs are advertised in newspapers and posted with minority organizations, as well as through internal agency bulletin boards.

What to Expect

The organization, which has an impressive record of achievement in the field of antipoverty work, continues to focus strongly and effectively on its mission. Applicants should be forewarned that PNCAA is said to offer very low starting salaries.

Potent Quote

"The group's basic constituency is best described as those who have historically been least able to win effective action from the economic structure through acting on their own: the homeless, low-income people, members of minority groups, the disabled, and seniors."

(Summary, BBP Services Newsletter, December, 1997.)

Rails to Trails Conservancy

1100 17th Street NW, 10th Floor, Washington, D.C. 20036
202/331-9696
World Wide Web: http://www.railtrails.org/
Contact: Karen Cicelski

Overview
Founded in 1986, Rails-to-Trails Conservancy (RTC) is a private non-profit organization that promotes the conversion of unused railroad corridors into trails.

By the Numbers
The organization boasts a membership base of approximately 70,000 people and supports field offices in 6 states—Florida, Michigan, Illinois, Ohio, Pennsylvania, and California. RTC has preserved almost 10,000 miles of trails, providing both transportation options and safe, accessible recreational use.

The Mission
RTC works to benefit U.S. communities by supporting the development of a national network of public trails from corridors and rail lines no longer used for rail traffic.

Words to the Wise
As of this writing, the organization's web site provides information on specific employment opportunities. The site also provides details about internships.

What to Expect

The group has accomplished a great deal in a very short period of time, and appears well positioned to take advantage of "an extensive network of contacts in the recreation, transportation and conservation communities."

Potent Quote

"RTC helps to create a national environment that promotes, protects and facilitates the process that has preserved almost 10,000 miles of precious natural resource.... RTC activities include notifying trail advocates and local governments of upcoming railroad abandonments; assisting public and private agencies in the complexities of trail corridor acquisition; providing technical assistance to private citizens as well as trail planners and managers on trail design, development and protection; and publicizing rail-trail issues throughout the country."

(From the organization's web site.)

Rainforest Action Network

> *221 Pine Street, Suite 500, San Francisco, California 94104*
> *415/398-4404*
> *Fax: 415/398-2732*
> *World Wide Web: http://www.ran.org/ran/*
> *Contact: Marie Hopper, Office Manager*

Overview
Virtually from the moment of its founding in 1985, the Rainforest Action Network (RAN) has been a major player in promoting the preservation of tropical rainforests. By mobilizing citizen protest and community action groups, and by supporting activists in tropical countries, RAN has helped to strengthen the international rainforest conservation movement. It is distinguished from similar groups devoted to the rainforest problem by its focus on grassroots education and networking resources, and by its ability to bring about quick direct action through consumer protest or non-violent site-specific activism when rainforests are threatened.

By the Numbers

Total Membership: 30,000.

RAN is supported by an extensive worldwide volunteer network of more than 150 Rainforest Action Groups (RAGs), RAN is dependent largely on member contributions; its member base includes supporters from around the world.

The Mission
As its name implies, the Rainforest Action Network is devoted to the protection and preservation of tropical rainforests. It also works to protect the rights of people living in and around those forests. RAN brings

the plight of rainforests and their inhabitants to public attention and organizes and mobilizes community action groups throughout the United States, using education, conferences, media campaigns, grass-roots organizing, and non-violent direct action.

Words to the Wise

Questions concerning employment openings may be forwarded to the San Francisco office. The organization is strongly oriented toward volunteer action; it does offer some internships.

What to Expect

The organization has set aggressive goals on an issue that many activists in the environmental movement (and quite a few others) consider both important and highly time-sensitive. It is likely to continue its high-visibility work and to receive support from dedicated employees, volunteers, and donors.

One major organizational objective is to "ensure the financial stability necessary to sustain current programs and support new initiatives" by establishing an endowment fund.

Potent Quote

"[The organization's program methods include:] educating citizens, consumers, and the media; conducting research and analysis; organizing direct action, e.g., letter-writing campaigns, petition drives, demonstrations; establishing coalitions with environmental, scientific, and grassroots groups worldwide; holding conferences and seminars; supporting economic alternatives to deforestation; facilitating coordination between U.S. and Third World organizers; providing technical and financial support to native communities and [non-governmental organizations] in rainforest countries."

(From the organization's web site.)

The Salvation Army

615 Slaters Lane, Alexandria, Virginia 22313
703/684-5500
Fax: 703/684-3478
World Wide Web: http://www.salvationarmyusa.org/
Contact: Doree De Jong

Overview

The Salvation Army is one of the best-known charitable organizations in the world. It is also one of the largest, with over 1.7 million volunteers contributing to its goals and services, and one of the oldest; U.S. service dates from 1880. The Army educates the public in its mission through the production and distribution of pamphlets and brochures. It also provides programs in Christian education and assists local chapters in the establishment of their own programs. However, it is primarily directed towards basic social services and the preaching of the Gospel, which it does in 160 languages in over 100 countries around the world. The Army is both an evangelical Protestant denomination and an international nonsectarian Christian organization.

By the Numbers

Staff: Approximately 40,000.

Budget: $1.4 billion.

The Salvation Army is divided into four territories: Western, Central, Southern, and Eastern, with national headquarters in Alexandria, Virginia, and international headquarters in London, England. Territories consist of smaller units known as divisions. Each territory in the United States functions as a tax-exempt corporation. Overall, income is derived from private contributions, government funds, fees for program services, sales of products, and the United Way and other foundations. The majority of the group's expenses is devoted to programs and services, while a smaller portion is committed to administration and fundraising.

The Mission

The Salvation Army works to provide assistance to all people in need, without regard to race, color or creed, using the Bible, and specifically the Gospel of Jesus Christ, as its foundation.

Words to the Wise

Although largely a volunteer organization, the Army does require a large number of skilled and dedicated employees to oversee its many different programs in hundreds of regions throughout the country.

What to Expect

The Salvation Army has adapted and enhanced the basic human services it has provided for over 130 years to meet more contemporary needs. New programs are continually being established to provide disaster relief, day care services, summer camps, assistance and care to senior citizens, medical facilities, shelters for abused wives and children, counseling services in a number of areas, vocational training, and drug rehabilitation. The Army has grown to accommodate the increasing changes and challenges posed by modern mores and technologies, cementing its importance as one of the leading organizations devoted to human services in the world.

Potent Quote

"The Salvation Army requires skilled and dedicated personnel to carry on its many-faceted programs. Employees are hired to perform clerical work in Salvation Army offices, to work in Salvation Army social service programs as professional case workers, [to] supervise and work in Salvation Army youth programs and boys' and girls' clubs, and [to] help in specialized fields...."

(From the organization's web site.)

San Diego Zoo

P.O. Box 551, San Diego, California 92112-0551
619/231-1515
619/557-3968 (Job line)
Contact: Human Resources
World Wide Web: http://www.sandiegozoo.org/

Overview
The San Diego Zoo is one of the world's leading animal conservation organizations. Established in 1916, the Zoo currently attracts over three million visitors annually. Its one hundred acres provides a home to over four thousand species, along with a Children's Zoo and a Botanical Garden. It has also established a Center for Reproduction of Endangered Species. The San Diego Zoo gained a great deal of needed publicity through the numerous appearances of its Goodwill Ambassador, Joan Embery, on the *Tonight Show*.

By the Numbers
Staff: 1,000.

Budget: $60,000,000.

The Zoo is essentially self-supporting, deriving 98 percent of its operating budget from gate receipts, zoo concessions, grants, and memberships. The remaining 2 percent comes from a city tax.

The Mission
The San Diego Zoo works to preserve and protect animal species and promote a greater understanding and appreciation of animals through exhibits, educational and research programs, and the application of modern and scientific methods to save animals from extinction.

Words to the Wise

The San Diego Zoo is part of the Zoological Society of San Diego, a private, nonprofit organization which also includes the San Diego Wild Animal Park and the Center for Reproduction of Endangered Species (CRES). Altogether, the Zoological Society employs more than 1,500 individuals. At the Zoo, 115 keepers care for over 3,800 animals, with many more hired as assistants and administrative support people. Acceptance as an intern can provide a foot in the door for future Zoo employment.

Employment at the San Diego Zoo comes with a number of perks, including free passes to the zoo for family and friends. All employees are welcome to attend departmental meetings, resulting in a great sense of community; a mentoring program is available to support those interested in making zoos a lifelong career.

What to Expect

The San Diego Zoo has been a the leader in the movement to make zoos more conservation- and education-oriented, and less of an environment where animals are confined in cages for public viewing. Old-style zoo management has become a thing of the past; instead of individual keepers, teams now care for specific animal species. The San Diego Wild Animal Park allows animals to roam freely in natural environments, while the humans who view them are "caged." Its work to save animal species from extinction, however, is what sets the San Diego Zoo apart and continues to earn it public and private support.

A love of animals, a desire to take part in important conservation efforts, and a willingness to put in long hours are prerequisites for those seeking employment at the Zoo.

Potent Quote

"People are viewing animals—as pets, in zoos, or for food—in different ways from before... We're starting to view animals as beings with emotions and feelings, and this will have an impact on the way we treat them."

(Curly Simerson, animal care manager for mammals at the San Diego Zoo, quoted in *Management Review*, August, 1995.)

Save the Children

82 Patton Avenue, 6th Floor, Ashville NC 28801
704/251-5204
World Wide Web: http://www.savethechildren.org/
Contact: Phyllis Stiles, Director

Overview

One of the most active and visible contemporary organizations devoted to improving the lives of children, Save the Children promotes early childhood education, economic opportunity, and emergency response campaigns on a global level.

By the Numbers

Contributions: $100 million.

Approximately 83 percent of all spending is devoted to "building the human and material resources needed to operate and sustain cost-effective programs on the ground."

The Mission

The group is committed to improving the health and well-being of children by working directly with families and communities. It places a special emphasis on improving the quality of life in families by assisting parents, especially mothers, and their children to attain the goals of physical health, economic security, and good education.

Words to the Wise

Questions concerning employment openings may be forwarded to the address at the head of this listing.

What to Expect

The organization is stable and has an exceptionally broad base of support. Its affiliation with celebrities like actress Sally Struthers and singer David Bowie and its strong and sustained fundraising presence in the media seem likely to ensure the continuation of its mission for many years to come.

The organization was recently given a "Top Five" rating by *Money* Magazine for sound financial management as a charitable organization.

Potent Quote

"We constantly evaluate and adapt programs to ensure that they are as effective as possible. In some cases, where we believe we cannot succeed, we phase out of programs. In all cases, lessons learned in one community are applied to, and tested in, programs around the world. Since we began working in 1932, we have learned from millions of families and children. We continue to share what we have learned so our programs are the best they can possibly be."

(From the organization's web site.)

Scripps Institution of Oceanography

University of California, San Diego, La Jolla, California 92093-0210
Human Resources: Mail Code 0967, La Jolla, California 92093-0967
619/534-2812
619/682-1000 (Job line)
Fax: 619/822-0547
World Wide Web: http://www-sio.ucsd.edu/
(For jobs: http://www-hr.ucsd.edu/~staffing/)
Contact: UCSD Human Resources

Overview

The Scripps Institution of Oceanography, one of the oldest, largest, and most important centers for research and graduate training in the marine sciences, has earned an impressive international reputation. Founded in 1903 as the Marine Biological Association, the Scripps Institution has been an integral part of the University of California since 1912. Since its founding it has been a leader in the field of marine life and habitats. Over the years, its scientific scope has grown beyond biological research to include physical, chemical, geological, and geophysical studies of the oceans.

By the Numbers

Staff: 1,200.

The Institution is currently conducting more than 300 research programs in areas as diverse as global warming, earthquake prediction, the marine food chain, and sea life as a source for pharmaceuticals.

The Mission

The organization's twofold mission is biological research and physical, geological, chemical, and geophysical studies of the oceans.

Words to the Wise

The Scripps Institution offers an ideal setting for future scientists who require intensive research training, as well as for laboratory technicians. For non-scientists, jobs are available in a number of areas, including executive, management, administrative, clerical, and technical. Employment applications are made through the Human Resources Office of the University of California, San Diego, in La Jolla, and can be submitted by walk-in visits at the Campus Employment Office (10280 North Torrey Pines Road, Suite 266, La Jolla), or by mail (see address at the beginning of this listing), fax, or e-mail (resume@ucsd.edu). There are also volunteer and internship opportunities.

As of this writing, the organization's web site gives information on current employment opportunities.

What to Expect

The Scripps Institution is financially stable and has enjoyed the support of numerous patrons over the years. It is a worldwide leader in the study of the biological and environmental impact of the oceans and marine life on our planet. Although it has been criticized in recent years for its promotion of such experiments as the Acoustic Thermometry of Ocean Climate program to measure global warming (which many critics claim could have a negative effect on marine life), the Institution's influence and reputation are sufficiently strong to ensure the vigorous pursuit of its mission.

Potent Quote

"For more than ninety years, scientists at Scripps have conducted a continuous search on the seas and in the laboratory for knowledge about the marine environment."

(From the organization's web site.)

The Sierra Club

85 Second Street, 2nd Floor, San Francisco, California 94105-3441
415/977-5500
Fax: 415/977-5799
Contact: Human Resources Department
World Wide Web: http://www.sierraclub.org /

Overview

The Sierra Club employs a combination of research, lobbying, education, community organizing, and publications to bring its message of conservation and preservation of natural resources to the public and to influence political and governmental decision making in the area of conservation. The club has lobbied for the preservation of ancient forests and for reform in public lands management. It has also played a key role in such initiatives as the Endangered Species Act, the Resource Conservation and Recovery Act (RCRA), the North American Free Trade Agreement (NAFTA), International Lending Reform, Clean Water/Wetland, and Population Stabilization.

By the Numbers

Staff: 375.

Budget: $35,000,00.

The Sierra Club is entirely supported by its members, with 65 chapters in every U.S. state and in Canada. The club also maintains numerous branch and affiliate offices throughout the country.

The Mission

By taking a proactive role in public policy decisions and legislative actions, the Sierra Club works to promote the conservation of our planet's environment.

Words to the Wise

In any given year, there can be between sixty and eighty staff openings for such positions as Organizer, Writer/Editor, Lobbyist, Media Rep, Field Organizer, Financial Analyst, Administrative Assistant, and Office Manager, as well as for basic office support staff. Part-time employees, interns, and volunteers are also sought. Jobs are advertised in both local and national newspapers, in specialized journals, and through employment agencies. As of this writing, information about job openings is available on the organization's web site.

What to Expect

As interest in environmental issues grows, the Sierra Club—one of the most influential and visible environmental groups—finds itself well positioned to extend its mission into the next century.

Potent Quote

"Our purpose is to explore, enjoy and protect the wild places of the earth; to practice and promote the responsible use of the earth's ecosystems and resources; to educate and enlist humanity to protect and restore the quality of the natural and human environments; and to use all lawful means to carry out these objectives."

(From the organization's mission statement.)

Trust for Public Land

> *116 New Montgomery, 4th Floor, San Francisco, California 94105*
> *415/495-4014 (Job line available through this number.)*
> *Contact: Human Resources Department*
> *World Wide Web: http://www.igc.org/tpl/*

Overview

Founded in 1972, the Trust for Public Land (TPL) works closely with private landowners, communities, and government agencies to conserve and protect over a thousand sites across the nation as parks, playgrounds, community gardens, recreation centers, and historic landmarks. The Trust uses land acquisition, financing, research, public education, lobbying, litigation, and training programs to achieve its goals. Half of TPL's resources are dedicated to improving metropolitan areas and broadening environmental initiatives by promoting urban open space issues.

By the Numbers

Staff: 180.

Budget: $18,000,000.

The Trust is funded primarily through land sales. The remainder comes from foundations (20 percent) and individual contributions (10 percent).

The Mission

The Trust for Public Land works on a national basis to ensure the conservation of land for all people to enjoy as parks, gardens, and natural areas. In partnership with government, business, and community groups, TPL acquires and preserves open space for human use, pioneers methods of environmentally sound land use and conservation, and publicizes information about nonprofit land acquisitions. Acquired land is protected for public use by means of conservation real estate, negotiation, public finance, and litigation.

Words to the Wise

One-third of TPL's staff are Project Managers. Administrative assistants, bookkeepers, attorneys, researchers, lobbyists, and fund raisers also make up a significant percentage of the work force. Interns are hired on occasion. There are usually a dozen or so staff openings a year. Jobs are advertised in newspapers and nonprofit journals, through mailing lists, and by college campus postings.

TPL works to promote ethnic diversity in the environmental movement, and stresses the same principle in its hiring practices.

What to Expect

TPL's effectiveness at promoting public and private action in a variety of settings is likely to continue to attract the interest and praise of business, government, and members of the public concerned about the issues of managed economic development, community revitalization, and environmental protection. In Baltimore, Mayor Kurt L. Schmoke stated that the Trust's "continuing collaboration with Baltimore city agencies is an example of a public-private partnership working to meet our city's needs."

Potent Quote

"At the invitation of local governments, TPL can move quickly to buy property for conservation, parks, and open space. We hold the land until public funds are available to purchase it. Then TPL sells the land to public agencies at or below fair market value— often covering the costs associated with the transaction."

(From the organization's web site.)

Union of Concerned Scientists

> *2 Brattle Square, Cambridge MA 02238-9105*
> *215/567-7000*
> *World Wide Web: http://www.ucsusa.org/*
> *Contact: Deputy Director of Development*

Overview

Founded in 1969, the Union of Concerned Scientists (UCS) is a nation-wide alliance of citizens and scientists concerned about the potential for the misuse of science and technology, and eager to channel scientific research efforts to constructive social purposes. The organization has helped to enact policies promoting the use of renewable energy; lobbied in favor of international agreements to address the global warming problem; and helped to strengthen safety standards at nuclear power plants.

By the Numbers

The organization boasts over 70,000 members. Through its "Sound Science Initiative," 1,500 scientists provide information on environmental science to key figures in the government and the media.

Words to the Wise

As of this writing, information on current job openings is featured on the organization's web site.

What to Expect

UCS's leadership rightly points out that the coming together of concerned citizens and esteemed scientists provides this organization with a unique outlook and mission.

The UCS has stressed the importance of working in coalition with other groups that share important objectives concerning the environment. This is likely to receive even more focus as environmental issues begin to dominate national and international attention in coming years.

Potent Quote

"The Union of Concerned Scientists (UCS) is a nonprofit organization of scientists and other citizens dedicated to advancing responsible public policies in areas where technology plays a critical role. UCS's efforts focus on global environmental issues, energy and transportation policy, biotechnology and sustainable agriculture, and nuclear proliferation."

(From the organization's web site.)

United Negro College Fund

> 8260 Willow Oaks, Corporate Drive, P.O. Box 10444, Fairfax VA 22031-4511
> 800/332-UNCF
> *World Wide Web: http://www.UNCF.org/*
> *Contact: Director of Human Resources*

Overview

Incorporated in 1944, the United Negro College Fund (UNCF) is an educational assistance organization comprising thirty-nine historically black colleges and universities—more than a third of all such institutions in the country. The colleges are located in ten southern states, in Texas, and in Ohio. Nearly 300,000 students have graduated from UNCF colleges.

UNCF is America's oldest and most respected support organization for higher education among minorities.

By the Numbers

UNCF offers over 450 programs—including scholarships, faculty development, technical assistance, and other campaigns—meant to strengthen the quality of education for students, faculty, and member colleges. Over 54,000 students now attend member institutions.

Annually, 30,000 volunteers assist with a large number of fundraising events. Since its inception, the organization has raised over $1 billion.

The Mission

UNCF raises funds, offers program services, and provides technical support to member colleges and the students who attend these institutions.

Words to the Wise
Questions concerning employment openings may be forwarded to the Fairfax office.

What to Expect
UNCF is widely regarded as one of the most effectively managed non-profit institutions in the country. It seems likely to continue to retain this status for the foreseeable future. The organization was recently named as the #1 educational organization in The Chronicle of Philanthropy's yearly survey of American charitable groups. Less than 13 cents out of every dollar raised in 1996 was used for fundraising activities; during the same period, less than 3 cents out of every dollar was used to support administration.

UNCF's most recent capital drive exceeded its goal of $250 million by 12 percent.

Potent Quote
"Using scholarships, internships, fellowships, research and study abroad opportunities, the College Fund and its member institutions have a unique ability to reach and educate minority and economically disadvantaged students, and to help prepare them for tomorrow's competitive work environment."

(From the organization's web site.)

United Way of America

> *701 North Fairfax Street, Alexandria, Virginia 22314-2045*
> *703/836-7000*
> *World Wide Web: http://www.unitedway.org/*
> *Contact: Dr. Kim Kitchen*

Overview

United Way of America is one of America's largest and best-known philanthropic organizations. It was established in 1887 to assist twenty-two other organizations in providing relief for people who had come to Denver, Colorado, to seek their fortune during the Colorado Gold Rush, and afterward had fallen on hard times. United Way has since grown into a national umbrella organization that supports the charitable work of more than 2,300 local United Way agencies. UWA provides marketing support and management assistance, helps to develop community partnerships and to train volunteers, and works with the local agencies to identify community needs, distribute funds, and disseminate information. UWA relies heavily on over 650,000 volunteers to help meet its goals, especially during its annual fund-raising drive. Each local United Way is an independent incorporated organization governed by area volunteers. In 1974, UWA created United Way International; there are now more than two hundred United Way organizations outside the United States.

By the Numbers

Staff: 196.

Two-thirds of United Way's income is received from member contributions in a single, sweeping fund-raising campaign each year. In 1994, local United Way agencies raised more than $3 billion from 80 million contributors to support the work of more than 41,000 health and social welfare programs. More than $2 billion of this amount resulted from member contributions within the workplace, while almost $800 million came from corporate donations. Of the income not allocated for distribution to other agencies, 85 percent goes to programs and services, the remainder to administrative costs and fund-raising.

The Mission

United Way of America seeks to help people help one another through its support and service to local United Way agencies. Local United Ways assess the needs of the community and distribute the money raised during the annual UWA fund drive to the non-profit organizations it has determined can best serve those needs. UWA also provides key assistance to its members in developing and promoting local programs, in training volunteers, and in advocating on behalf of social service programs at all levels.

Words to the Wise

Questions concerning employment openings at the organization's headquarters may be forwarded to the Alexandria office.

What to Expect

The United Way encourages a work environment where staff members are enthusiastic, motivated, and firmly dedicated to UWA principles. As responsibility for the welfare of those in need has shifted from the federal to the state level, UWA has had a growing influence on the development of social programs. The parent organization is working to provide increased fund-raising assistance and training to local agencies, focusing especially on the responsible dispensation of funds. This is a crucial shift, since UWA's success has often been measured by the total monies it has raised rather than the best possible application of those monies. Many local agencies are refocusing their efforts to meet the most significant needs of the community and its families. UWA will also seek to improve media coverage of its efforts and will step up promotional campaigns to increase public awareness of its work and value to each locality. Finally, UWA wants to achieve a greater diversity in all areas of operation, including fund-raising and distribution, communications, recruitment of employees and volunteers, and training at all levels. The creation of a "Young Leaders Society" by local United Way agencies is intended to encourage young professionals to become more involved in the United Way's work, by helping to raise money and by volunteering for community projects. UWA hopes that these and other initiatives will encourage its local agencies to take a more active role in developing programs that benefit their communities.

Potent Quote

"At United Way of America, we realize that the time to focus our energies and those of our system is now, and we have spent the past year working with our members to redefine who we are and what we must do to become the primary force in building stronger communities.... We are now deeply engaged in reworking United Way of America's internal strategic plan to ensure that our efforts are devoted to assisting our members to enhance their fundraising and demonstrate their community-wide impact."

(From the organization's web site.)

The Urban Institute

> *2100 M Street NW, Washington, D.C. 20037*
> *202/857-8709*
> *World Wide Web: http://www.urban*
> *Contact: Personnel Office*

Overview

Founded in 1968, the Urban Institute (UI) examines both the social and economic difficulties facing the United States and the programs and policies designed to resolve them.

By the Numbers

Staff: Over 250.

Employees work in 9 policy research centers, where they "identify and measure the extent of social problems, assess developing trends and solutions to those problems, evaluate existing social and economic programs and policy options, and offer conceptual clarification and technical assistance in the development of new strategies."

The Mission

The Institute's goals include: focusing thinking about what works—and what doesn't—in efforts to combat social problems; helping policy makers develop and implement better programs; and heightening general awareness about issues and initiatives affecting the public interest.

Words to the Wise

As of this writing, the organization's web site features information about a number of current job openings, many of which are research- or computer-related.

What to Expect

Historically, UI has been strongly associated with analyses of national trends in the social and economic arena, and with its evaluation of national policy questions. In recent years, however, the organization has put an increasingly heavy emphasis on the job of assessing the effectiveness of initiatives at the local, state, and regional levels. This trend is likely to continue, as is UI's emerging commitment to helping nations in Eastern Europe and the former Soviet Union evaluate various policies and initiatives.

Potent Quote

"Ultimately, for the Urban Institute, solving the puzzle means performing an essential role in a democratic society: bringing accuracy, objectivity, and insight to bear on the way the nation looks at problems and their proposed solutions."

(From the organization's web site.)

Veterans of Foreign Wars
of the United States

406 West 34th Street, Kansas City, Missouri 64111
816/756-3390
Fax: 816-968-1157
World Wide Web: http://www.vfw.org/
Contact: Bob Greene

Overview

Veterans of Foreign Wars of the United States (originally American Veterans of Foreign Service, and commonly known as the VFW) was founded in 1899 by a group of Spanish American War veterans seeking rights and benefits related to their service. The organization has grown since then to include veterans of the Philippine Insurrection, World Wars I and II, the Korean and Vietnam wars, and any overseas conflict in which a campaign medal was awarded. With over 2.1 million members, the VFW promotes American patriotism through educational programs, publications, youth activities, service to the community, charity work, and fund-raising. The organization works on a legislative level to ensure adequate care for veterans in a number of areas, including health, retirement, disability, and training.

By the Numbers

Staff: 290.

Budget: $23,900,000.

The Mission

The VFW is an organization of overseas veterans committed to preserving and strengthening a spirit of friendship among its members through acts of assistance to veterans or to their widows and orphans, and by honoring those who have fallen in foreign wars. The VFW also works to foster patriotism and to preserve and defend the United States from foreign aggression. It supports maximum military strength to achieve national security.

Words to the Wise
Questions concerning employment openings at the headquarters may be forwarded to the Kansas City office.

What to Expect
The VFW is currently facing demographic challenges. A decline in foreign conflicts requiring U.S. involvement, along with a variety of changes in society in large, has left the VFW short of young people to take over leadership positions within the organization. The average VFW member is about 73 years old and often unable to take part in meetings and fund drives. Local posts are also diminishing in size and stature. The organization is attempting to reach out to a younger constituency in order to recruit the newer, younger members it needs to thrive in the future. Outreach includes sending teams to military posts and conflicts in order to distribute CARE packages, letters, and postcards, and the organization of ceremonies to greet military servicemen and women upon their return to the U.S.

Potent Quote
"The Veterans of Foreign Wars is an association of overseas veterans dedicated to preserve and strengthen comradeship among its members, to assist worthy comrades, to perpetuate the memory and history of our dead and to assist their widows and orphans, to maintain true allegiance to the government of the United States of America, to foster true patriotism and to preserve and defend the United States from all of her enemies."

(From the organization's web site.)

W. Alton Jones Foundation, Inc.

232 East High Street, Charlottesville, Virginia 22902-5178
804/295-2134
Fax: 804/295-1648
World Wide Web: http://www.wajones.org/
Contact: Judith Carlin

Overview

The W. Alton Jones Foundation is a charitable organization that awards grants to organizations and programs seeking to improve the quality of life on earth in accordance with the Foundation's own goals. It focuses in particular on the conservation of natural resources, environmental protection, peace, and arms control. Its numerous grantmaking programs include The Sustainable World Program and The Secure World Program. Each is governed by a restricted set of program initiatives, and grassroots support for certain organizations.

By the Numbers

In 1996, the Foundation awarded 308 grants amounting to over $20 million.

The Mission

The W. Alton Jones Foundation is a private grant-making foundation focusing on worldwide environmental protection. The Foundation's goals are to provide protection to the earth's life-support systems—and by so doing, to develop new ways for humanity to take responsible stewardship of the planet's ecological systems—and to eliminate nuclear warfare as a planetary possibility by working to achieve alternative methods for the resolution of conflicts, and by promoting a more secure world overall. Grants and seed money are awarded to qualified organizations submitting proposals for projects and programs that work towards this end.

Words to the Wise

Although the organization may be of significant interest to those interested in pursuing philanthropic environmental and peace career opportunities, the staff appears to be small, and openings, when they arise, are likely to be highly competitive.

What to Expect

The organization is stable and highly respected within the philanthropic community.

Potent Quote

"The Sustainable World Program supports efforts that will ensure that human activities do not undermine the quality of life of future generations and do not erode the earth's capacity to support living organisms. The foundation addresses this challenge with a tight focus on issues whose resolution will determine how habitable the planet remains over the next century and beyond: maintaining biological diversity; ensuring that human economic activity is based on sound ecological principles; solving humanity's energy needs in environmentally sustainable ways; and avoiding patterns of contamination that erode the planet's capacity to support life.... The Secure World Program seeks to build a secure world, free from the nuclear threat. The foundation addresses this challenge by: promoting Common Security and strategies related to how nations can structure their relationships without resorting to nuclear weapons; [and] devising and promoting policy options to control and eventually eliminate existing nuclear arsenals and fissile materials...."

(From the organization's web site.)

Western States Center

P.O. Box 40305, Portland OR 97240
503/228-8866
Fax: 503/228-1865
World Wide Web: http://www.igc.org/westernstates/
Contact: Personnel Department

Overview

The Western States Center is a regional, progressive organization consisting of community leaders, elected officials and political activists from eight Western states: Idaho, Alaska, Montana, Nevada, Oregon, Utah, Washington and Wyoming. Western States Center seeks to bolster a progressive political agenda in the west and to create innovative and successful organizing efforts. It provides support to community-based organizations and helps to build statewide policy coalitions. The organization conducts research and policy analyses, trains grassroots organizers and community leaders in advocacy skills and public policy, provides consulting services on education and organizing campaigns, as well as strategy and organizational development, and encourages political leaders with a progressive agenda to run for political office.

By the Numbers

The Center gets funding from private grants as well as from individual donations.

The Mission

The Western States Center promotes citizen action and leadership and provides advocacy and support in social, economic, and environmental issues affecting the public. The organization seeks to establish an effective progressive movement in the West that upholds values of equality, justice, and democracy, and supports new generations of progressive public leaders who pursue an agenda of social and economic justice.

Words to the Wise
Questions about employment opportunities may be forwarded to the Portland office.

What to Expect
The Center is well positioned to continue pursuing its goals through the development of key programs in which community leaders, activists, and organizers are developed. Emerging leaders are identified and assisted in broadening their skills and experience; coalitions are formed to address key issues in the West; research and organization are applied to economic issues to find ways of both promoting jobs and protecting the environment; and investigations are conducted into campaign financing in an effort to create a more inclusive democracy.

Potent Quote
"The Western States Center was founded in 1987 to challenge the isolation felt by many progressives, and to help stimulate creative and successful organizing efforts in the West."

(From the organization's web site.)

WGBH Educational Foundation

125 Western Avenue, Boston, Massachusetts, 02134
617/492-2777
Jobline: 617/492-2777, ext. 3742
World Wide Web: http://www.boston.com/wgbh
Contact: Michael Enwright, Human Resources

Overview

Boston's WGBH (Channel 2) is one of the leading public broadcasting institutions in the United States, producing a sizable chunk of all programming for the PBS network. The Western Avenue facility also incorporates a second television station, WGBX (channel 44), and an FM radio station (89.7).

By the Numbers

Staff: 750

Budget: $128 million.

WGBH is one of the largest and most prestigious public stations in the country. As of this writing, a campaign to reduce public television funding as a whole has been underway in Washington for some time; the station has responded to this challenge with equally strong initiatives aimed at the development of new funding sources.

The Mission

WGBH is an educational foundation; its television and radio operations are dedicated to delivering quality educational and cultural programming to Boston-area viewers and listeners. Through its production of such programs as "Nova," "Frontline," and "This Old House," the station also addresses national educational and cultural programming needs.

Words to the Wise

WGBH relies on fund raisers for a large portion of its revenue stream; some staff members begin their careers in a fund-raising capacity. One common means of entry to the organization is through a paid tele-marketing position, contacting lapsed or soon-to-lapse donors to suggest upgrades and renewal gifts. Those with strong marketing and/or business experience in the private sector may have a good chance at mid-level and supervisory positions in the development area. Applicants with strong technical skills are also likely to have a distinct edge, as the station seeks to solidify its position in a rapidly growing (and often unpredictable) telecommunications environment.

WGBH is one of the most respected producers of television programming in the country. Not surprisingly, production-related openings are highly competitive. Unless you have superior qualifications and a good deal of luck, you will probably find that "prestige" jobs (those on the production side) are hard to land. Extensive broadcast experience is essential, and even then the odds against entry are likely to be formidable. The likeliest means of entry to the foundation's workforce appears to be through positions unrelated to broadcast production.

As of this writing, information about current employment opportunities is accessible through the organization's web site.

What to Expect

The station represents an important piece of the national public broadcasting system, and it places a strong emphasis on high quality and personal accountability. Its focus on the consistent delivery of results makes WGBH a demanding but rewarding place to work.

Despite its stability and reputation, WGBH faces a number of serious challenges over the next decade. The efforts of many in Congress to zero out public television funding entirely have made front-page news, but WGBH also faces major questions about the nature of its operations. Can it simultaneously hold on to its audience in a competitive market, retain its sense of mission, manage ongoing political pressures, and operate with greater attentiveness than ever to bottom-line issues? The successful employee at WGBH will be both sensitive to the revenue requirements of a major broadcast production center and committed to the foundation's long-term mission.

Potent Quote

"The purpose of this not-for-profit corporation is to promote the general education of the public by offering television, radio, and other telecommunications programs and services that inform, inspire, and entertain, so that persons of all ages, origins, and beliefs may be encouraged, in an atmosphere of artistic freedom, to learn and appreciate the history, the sciences, the humanities, the practical arts, the music, the politics, the economics, and other significant aspects of the world they live in, and thereby to enrich and improve their lives."

(From the preamble of the organization's bylaws.)

Whitney Museum of Art

---

945 Madison Avenue, New York, New York 10021
212/570-3645
World Wide Web: http//www.echonyc.com/~whitney/
Contact: Human Resources

Overview
The Whitney Museum of Art is one of the world's premier museums. It is located in midtown Manhattan in an acclaimed building designed by Marcel Breuer in 1966.

By the Numbers
The museum is over 150 years old. A major upcoming exhibit, "The American Century—Art and Culture, 1900-2000," which is scheduled to open in April 1999, features over seven hundred works from the visual and the performing arts, architecture and design, film, and literature. A branch museum, the Whitney at Phillip Morris, occupies a Park Avenue space of 1,000 square feet.

The Mission
The Whitney Museum of Art is dedicated to the exhibition of twentieth-century art and to the promotion of contemporary American artists.

Words to the Wise
Applying for an internship is one good way to become eligible for a permanent position. Up to thirty internships a year are offered, covering such responsibilities as curating, assistance in educational and communications programs, and publications. Internships vary in length from nine weeks to four months, and are generally reserved for college juniors and seniors. An art history/fine arts background is required.

Information on regular job openings can be obtained by going directly to the museum and consulting the job posting book located at the information desk. The organization's web site requests that applicants not place phone calls or send e-mail regarding employment opportunities.

What to Expect

The Whitney Museum has worked to keep up with technological advances while maintaining curatorial and educational goals for great works of art. It has recently entered into a collaboration with NTT Corporation to produce a multimedia overview of twentieth-century American art, a presentation utilizing Super High Definition (SHD) imaging. This multimedia package is used primarily for fund-raising purposes, but it marks an important step forward in the application of modern technology to traditional art. With the Whitney's firm commitment to exploring the relationship between emerging technologies and the arts, it has positioned itself for a future leadership role in the field.

Potent Quote

"Artists don't work in a vacuum; there's an interaction between media and the times."

(Thelma Golden, curator, quoted in *Black Enterprise*, February 1996.)

The Wilderness Society

> 900 17th Street NW, Washington, D.C. 20006
> 202/833-2300
> *Contact: Employment Office*
> *World Wide Web: http://www.wilderness.org/*

Overview

The Wilderness Society (TWS) was founded in 1935, when a small group of conservationists banded together to work to preserve wild areas of the country before they were developed into extinction. The Society has played a historic role in the movement to save the nation's wilderness from extinction; its most notable success was probably the 1964 Wilderness Act, which enabled Congress to set aside selected areas in national forests, parks, wildlife refuges, and other federal lands that are not to be changed by humankind in any way (i.e., no roads, structures, vehicles, or other incursions that might affect the environment). TWS has also been instrumental in the passage of key bills in several states that protect natural resources.

By the Numbers

TWS derives a large portion of its funding from member contributions. With a 17 percent increase in membership in 1996, the Society appears to be in good financial shape.

As a direct or indirect result of TWS's efforts over the years, the American people currently enjoy approximately 104 million acres of protected wilderness.

The Mission

TWS is dedicated to preserving the wilderness and its wildlife and protecting American forests parks, rivers, deserts, and shorelands.

Words to the Wise

Questions concerning employment opportunities may be forwarded to the Washington office.

What to Expect

Effective action toward environmental protection remains a challenging mission for TWS, as for other conservation groups. In recent years, however, TWS has enjoyed progress and success on a number of fronts. With its current work in the Sierra Nevada and the Northern Forest of New England, TWS is continuing to work toward its goals of creating regional networks of protected wilderness and promoting an American land ethic.

Potent Quote

"Our key campaigns are Wild Alaska, Wilderness, and National Forests, along with programs that aim to ensure healthy management of our national parks, national wildlife refuges, and the lands managed by the Bureau of Land Management.... We're here to protect the land—your land—for now and for future generations."

(From the organization's web site.)

World Game Institute

3215 Race Street, Philadelphia PA 19104
215/387-0220
Fax: 215/387-3009
World Wide Web: http://www.worldgame.org/
Contact: Personnel Department

Overview

Founded in 1972 under the leadership of inventor and writer R. Buckminster Fuller, World Game Institute envisions itself as a "creative problem solving tool" providing a variety of educational tools that highlight global problems and their potential solutions. Group simulations known as World Game Workshops are an important part of the group's work.

The group is a Non-Governmental Organization affiliate of the United Nations.

By the Numbers

World Game Institute is a member of 6 prestigious educational/advocacy organizations.

The Mission

World Game Institute aims to offer the perspective and facts necessary to resolve important problems facing global society at the dawn of the twenty-first century. Its products and programs, which now include a variety of computer-related applications, are meant to help participants evaluate and address global and regional challenges from a planetary perspective.

Numbers count for a great deal at this organization, which tries to maintain "the world's most comprehensive inventory of global statistics on resources, production, human needs and trends, and opportunities for sustainable development." World Game Institute's seven key organizational goals include: the development of experience-based learning tools that put participants "in charge of the world"; the collection of important information about the planet's health and well being; the production of computer-related resources for a wide variety of users; the development and evaluation of problem-solving techniques; the development of educational materials that highlight global awareness; the promotion of World Game Workshops to a variety of audiences; and the wide distribution of the organization's programs as part of an ongoing effort to increase the input of citizens in the establishment of local and international policy.

Words to the Wise
Questions concerning employment openings may be forwarded to the Philadelphia office.

What to Expect
Over the years, the organization's activities to promote global awareness, and its efforts to reach out to key figures in government, business, and the media, have been rewarded with increasing respect and cooperation in these arenas. That trend is likely to continue.

Potent Quote

> *"World Game Workshops:* [We offer] versions for students, community groups, and corporations. Bring one to your community to educate about world issues, the environment, cultural awareness, and gender issues."

(From the organization's web site.)

World Wildlife Fund/
The Conservation Foundation

1250 24th Street, NW, Washington, D.C. 20037
202/293-4800
202/861-8350 (Job line)
World Wide Web: http://www.wwf.org/
Contact: Personnel Department

Overview

The World Wildlife Fund (WWF) and the Conservation Foundation (CF) affiliated with each other in 1985, combining finances, administration, and communications while keeping their conservation programs separate. Both organizations use training and technical assistance, direct action, research, community resources, human services, public education, and publications to pursue their initiatives, which have included studies of the American continent's wetlands and Great Lakes, programs for land use and community development, energy conservation in the Third World, campaigns to save endangered species, and numerous debt-for-nature swaps. Newsletters, public service announcements, multi-media exhibits, and direct mail appeals further the group's education commitment. WWF/CF also exerts pressure and influence on government agencies and private corporations to integrate and enforce conservation policies. In addition to its Washington headquarters, the combined group maintains an office in Gland, Switzerland, and has twenty-three affiliates on the North American continent. The international scope of its operation makes it unique among conservation organizations.

By the Numbers

Staff: 320 (WWF).

Budget: $45,000,000 (WWF); $4-5,000,000 (CF).

Funding for both organizations comes from a large number of sources, including individual donors, foundations, corporations, publications and films, royalties, investments, and the government. Almost 90 percent of income is poured into programs and services, with the remainder going to fund-raising and administrative costs.

The Mission
The WWF/CF works globally to preserve and protect the wilderness and endangered wildlife, with a major focus on tropical forest conservation in Latin America. The Conservation Fund's goals are to improve the overall quality of the environment and to ensure safe and wise use of the planet's natural resources. Both affiliated organizations seek to foster worldwide conservation awareness, to preserve diversity and life abundance on the planet, to create healthy ecological systems, and to foster endurable use of natural and biological resources.

Words to the Wise
There are approximately fifty staff openings a year, advertised in newspapers and via mailing lists.

What to Expect
The organization's size, international scope, and focus on a wide variety of wildlife and wildlands issues make it unique. Its mission is likely to be perceived by donors and members of the general public as more and more important in coming years.

Potent Quote

"We are uniquely positioned to act quickly when conservation emergencies arise, such as the need to save a highly endangered species or habitat or to acquire valuable land for a park or protected area."

(From the organization's web site.)

Zero Population Growth

> *1400 16th Street NW, Suite 320, Washington, D.C. 20036*
> *202/332-2200 or 1-800-767-1956*
> *Fax: 202/332-2302*
> *Contact: Human Resource Department*
> *World Wide Web: http://www.zpg.org/*

Overview
Since its founding in 1968, Zero Population Growth (ZPG) has become the nation's largest grassroots organization devoted to issues of population growth and its impact on the earth.

By the Numbers
ZPG is a member-based organization with 20 chapters nationwide and strong grassroots support, thanks to over 55,000 members and a national network of activists.

The Mission
Based on the premise that the planet's resources are finite and cannot support an infinite number of people, ZPG works to slow population growth throughout the world and achieve a sustainable balance of people and resources, as well as a safe environment. ZPG also seeks to educate the public about the effect of overpopulation on the world's natural resources and environments, and the quality of life of its inhabitants. The organization holds that unless population growth is significantly slowed, it will be impossible to address such critical issues as pollution, climate change, the extinction of animal species, the depletion of natural resources, urban development, and the health and welfare of present and future generations.

Words to the Wise

ZPG offers numerous volunteer and internship opportunities. Volunteers may perform a wide variety of functions—from staffing an information table to presenting ZPG's message to the public through speaking engagements at schools, community gatherings, and other channels. Numerous internships are offered in grassroots organizing, public speaking, legislation monitoring, media and communications, research, education, and fund-raising. Interns assist the staff and gain valuable experience leading to possible later employment. As of this writing, information regarding ZPG's internship program may be accessed via the organization's web site.

What to Expect

The organization appears well positioned to continue circulating the message that rapid population growth is a major contributor to environmental and social problems around the globe, and to pursue media campaigns, advocacy, and public endorsement of policies and legislation that help to lower birth rates. The group will continue its work on behalf of the creation of a society that is both healthy and self-sustaining.

Potent Quote

"Zero Population Growth is the nation's largest grassroots organization concerned with the impacts of rapid population growth and wasteful consumption. Continued population growth is foremost among the factors aggravating critical environmental and social problems."

(From the organization's web site.)

Zoo Atlanta

800 Cherokee Avenue, Atlanta, Georgia, 30315
404/624-5600
Jobline: (main number; follow prompts for job updates)
World Wide Web: http://www.zooatlanta.org
Contact: Human Resources Department

Overview

Ten years ago, Atlanta's zoo was rated as one of the worst in the country. Today it is one of the nation's finest. This extraordinary turn-around was the result of strong leadership, dedicated corporate sponsors (including Coca-Cola, Delta, and Ford) and a strong sense of civic pride among the citizens of Atlanta.

By the Numbers

Staff: 130

Budget: $10 million.

Zoo Atlanta now enjoys exceptional stability in its budget—and this after the organization made a strategic decision to rely entirely on private-sector and self-generated funding. The zoo receives no government support whatever. All its revenue comes from gate receipts, concessions sales, and private or corporate gifts. Zoo Atlanta has made a public commitment to continue operations only if it can do so as a top-tier facility capable of sustaining itself through private channels. Community outreach is a key part of this bold and successful strategy. Connection with the community and steady, solid growth are the hallmarks of today's Zoo Atlanta.

The Mission

Zoo Atlanta is a private, not-for-profit wildlife park committed to the exhibition, maintenance, breeding, and conservation of exotic and endangered animals. The zoo's goal is to entertain, educate, and enlighten the public in areas of wildlife preservation and management. Through its strong education and outreach programs, it brings a personal, hands-on wildlife experience to children and adults who would otherwise have very little experience with the animal world. The zoo works to supply real-life exposure to animals that are normally only seen on TV, incorporating all the visitor's senses into the experience. The zoo's efforts are meant to remind visitors of the status of wild animals as fellow residents of the planet.

Words to the Wise

Biology and the animal sciences offer the best natural routes of entry into the organization's animal-care work. Because of the prestige the zoo has earned over the past decade, however, entry-level positions in animal care are highly competitive. The public nature of the work favors applicants with strong interpersonal skills and an outgoing manner. Some specialization in avians, large animals, primates, or reptiles and amphibians is a plus.

To further its mission, the zoo sponsors a variety of excellent education and outreach programs. Those with a background in early childhood education and a good rapport with animals may well find opportunities in this area.

Finance and accounting areas also provide many entry-level and mid-level opportunities. Experience in the nonprofit sector is not necessarily required; in fact, private sector business experience can be a plus. Exciting opportunities also exist in the areas of marketing and public relations.

What to Expect

The future for Zoo Atlanta looks bright. The hard work of the past decade has built a broad and loyal base of support. Strong corporate sponsorships and a sense of a shared destiny with the community all seem to spell long-term stability.

One of the most serious challenges facing the zoo is the loss of its most valuable commodity: the animals. Many of its most important residents are nearly extinct in the wild. Some species have irretrievably depleted populations, and their only hope lies in captive breeding. Zoo Atlanta is already active in this area, and expects to place even more emphasis upon it in the future.

Potent Quote

"Zoo Atlanta is a wildlife park and zoological trust empowered to exhibit, interpret, study and care for wildlife in superior environments, to conserve biodiversity throughout the world, to enlighten and entertain the public, and to contribute to the cultural life of the community."

(From the organization's web site.)

Appendix A:
The Nonprofit
Job Search

Getting a Job with a Nonprofit

Working in the nonprofit sector used to carry a certain stigma. Somehow it was assumed that nonprofit jobs were more of a calling than a career. Not-for-profit companies were regarded as courts of last resort for those who couldn't find a job out in the "real" working world.

Not any more! The tables have turned, and this previously unrewarding market has now become very attractive to job-seekers—and for good reason. As more of the larger, profit-making organizations downsize, and more government jobs are cut back, the nonprofit sector offers increasing opportunities for people seeking to expand their career horizons. Jobs have opened up at every level of job-seeking, from clerical to professional. Nonprofits also often provide many benefits that corporate and government jobs do not—including a strong sense of doing something meaningful and helpful, and freedom from that focus on the bottom line that creates such pressure and stress in the corporate world.

One unfortunate stigma does remain. Jobs in the nonprofit sector do pay less on average than those in other sectors—approximately 25 percent less, in fact. But the rewards often outweigh the reduced pay. Many people who go to work in the nonprofit sector do so because they want to make a commitment to helping others in some way. Others do it because the work dynamics are more appealing than those found in corporate or government jobs. Particularly attractive is the strong sense of teamwork arising from a sense of shared missions and goals. And many enjoy the increased responsibilities of jobs that require employees to wear different hats and come up with innovative ideas and solutions. It promotes a kind of creativity that would most likely be stifled in another job sector. But be forewarned: It can also lead to a heavier workload and some pretty intense workdays.

Whatever their reasons may be for choosing to work for a nonprofit organization, those who make the conscious decision to leap to this sector from the corporate or government arenas have generally ended up happier and more fulfilled in their work. The potential rewards are great and the disappointments few and far between. Despite the salary reduction accompanying the move, quality of life can often improve greatly, and for many that is the most important factor of all in choosing a job.

It should be said, however, that nonprofit jobs are not for everybody. Some people are happier in a more structured environment where they are required to be in a certain place at a certain time and do certain things according to certain policies and procedures, period. Others lack the multi-faceted skills required by many nonprofit positions—expertise in fund-raising, for example, which requires specialized knowledge. And many simply prefer the higher rate of pay in the corporate and government sectors. Salary can be the biggest drawback to nonprofit work. In 1995, the median annual for a nonprofit executive was $54,095—a major comedown from the three-figure salaries drawn by their counterparts in the for-profit world.

Not that higher-paying jobs don't exist in the nonprofit sector. Some large and popular organizations can afford to pay competitive wages, thanks to celebrity support and well-timed publicity. As a rule, the larger the organization, the better the salary, just as in the private sector. But most nonprofit organizations operate well out of the public spotlight, and they are scraping by on extremely low budgets—often less than $100,000 a year. This is partly because public awareness of their good and serious work can get buried under the avalanche of publicity granted to the more "glamorous" nonprofits; but there can also be a misconception that those who work for nonprofit organizations are nonprofessionals who are working for the cause, not the pay. Such beliefs can drastically affect the level of donations received by the typical nonprofit company, as well as the quality of the employees it can hire. Few people realize how great an organization's expenses are and how much money is needed to keep it going. If the inability to pay a decent wage and benefits keeps qualified people from going to work there, a nonprofit with a good cause and a strong mission can easily go under.

For this reason the inequity of pay can have far-reaching effects, particularly when it comes to an organization's stability. The person who chooses to work in the nonprofit sector does so amid fears that cutbacks or failure of the mission could eliminate the job altogether. This risk, however, is also very much present in the corporate sector—the very reason that many people are now turning to the nonprofit arena. As this arena is increasingly recognized as a source of interesting, challenging, and fulfilling career opportunities, funding and salaries are gradually moving upwards, making it that much more accessible to all.

So how do you know whether nonprofit work is for you? You can start by being clear about what you want from your work. Self-examination is important in any personal decision you make, and it is especially important in a job search, where so many factors can come into play. How big an organization do you want to work for? What expertise do you have that can be specifically applied to nonprofit work? What do you envision yourself doing, and what personal and professional goals are you hoping to achieve? How well do you understand the needs and problems of nonprofit organizations? How passionate are you about causes and commitments? What are the ways in which you can make a difference? These are the kinds of questions you want to ask yourself before you plunge into the nonprofit sector. Once you feel sure of yourself and know this is the right market for you and your talents—you can begin your search!

Launching the Search

So where do you start? First, you probably need to identify what kind of work you want to tackle. Nonprofit work falls into two main categories. The first is program work—also known as the "front line." If you're a program worker, you're somebody with the particular skills, training, or education needed to perform the tasks that are the foundation of the organization. Typical program employees include counselors, social workers, therapists, educators, health service providers, researchers, disaster relief specialists, crisis interventionists, and so on. The second area is the infrastructure of the organization—the support system needed to keep the program workers in business. This area includes fund raising, accounting, public relations, management, general office support, etc., and provides the most employment opportunities for those who do not possess the necessary background for a front-line position. Please be aware, however, that fund raising in the nonprofit sector is a specialty in itself. Whatever fund-raising experience you may have acquired while working in the government or corporate sectors is unlikely to be transferable to a nonprofit position. The same goes for management skills. Many colleges and universities now offer graduate-level programs in nonprofit management, and this is worth investigating if managing is the area you hope to enter.

One of your strongest tools for finding a job in the nonprofit sector is probably networking. Entry into the world of nonprofits often comes through someone you know. If you don't know anybody, never fear. There are any number of ways you can make the right contacts. Start with your own close network of friends and acquaintances and spread the word that you are looking for a job with a nonprofit organization. You never know who might know somebody who is looking for a good employee. You can also research and, if possible, become involved with a community or professional organization in your vicinity. Ask to attend their meetings or try to arrange an information-gathering interview with somebody who is doing the sort of work in which you are interested. Learn as much as you can about the particular field, company, and position in which you are interested, and use that information when asking for referrals and further information. A clear demonstration of what you know and what you are willing to do will make a strong impression on the people you talk to, and they are more likely to remember you when a job opening arises.

Check your local library for listings of nonprofit associations and their phone numbers. Many organizations also publish newsletters, complete with job postings and the names of key individuals in that sector; if you're interested in a particular organization, you will probably want to call and ask for a copy to be mailed to you. Best of all, if you own or have access to a computer, you can use it to monitor newsgroups and e-mail lists that are likely to post announcements of job openings. One Usenet newsgroup you might want to try is **soc.org.nonprofits**.

Make the most of your computer resources. If you spot something on a mailing list or in a newsgroup that interests you and has some pertinence to your job search, send an e-mail to the person who posted it; he or she may turn out to be your key contact! Remember: The more feelers you put out, and the more referrals you get by doing your networking homework, the more likely you are to reach a somebody who has the job you want to apply for.

One way of networking that is unique to the nonprofit sector is volunteerism. Because so many nonprofit organizations have limited budgets, they tend to rely heavily on volunteers for all sorts of tasks, from stuffing envelopes to fund-raising. Volunteering can provide excellent opportunities for you *and* for the organization you'd like to work for, especially if that company is not presently hiring. Offer to volunteer a few hours of your time each week or each month. It will enable you to network more closely with key people, get to know the organization better as a potential place of work, and monitor employment opportunities as they arise. Most importantly, you'll be able to demonstrate your interest in and dedication to the organization's mission, and the particular gifts you would bring to it. This can go a long way toward getting you noticed and putting you first in line when a desirable position opens up.

Standard avenues to explore when looking for job postings include your local newspapers and periodicals like the Chronicle of Philanthropy and Philanthropy Journal. The Internet is another rich source of information about job openings. These resources are described in more detail in Appendix B.

Because jobs are limited and often require special skills and experience, organizations tend to promote from within rather than hire from the outside when it comes to management and executive positions. You may have to be willing to start in an entry-level position and work your way up. Actually, this has its rewards. As you learn about a nonprofit business from the bottom, you'll find opportunities for personal growth and rapid advancement that the private sector just doesn't offer, by and large. Many nonprofit executives started out as telemarketers or office workers and quickly worked their way to the top.

For budgetary reasons, nonprofit organizations often offer part-time as well as full-time jobs. Willingness to take a part-time job is another effective way of moving up in the company. It is also an ideal avenue for people who have limited schedules, or who are just returning to the job market and want to develop their skills before venturing into full-time work.

If you are currently attending a college, university, graduate school, or even high school, consider doing an internship. This may be your best bet for entering the nonprofit market. Interning enables you to learn more about the field and the organization you're interested in and to acquire the skills that will help you snag a job once you graduate. Like volunteering, interning is also a useful way to demonstrate what you are capable of doing. Many organizations prefer to hire people who have done internships with them and who therefore come with proven skills and experience for the work. The lengths and terms of internships vary from organization to organization, so you will need to do some research to figure out what best fits your interests and your schedule. Be warned, however, that it is often difficult to obtain an internship. Because most organizations will accept only a limited number of students, competition can be fierce.

Finally, when applying for jobs within the nonprofit sector, remember that some things are not all that different from the private and government sectors. Use the same standards of excellence as you would use for any job in creating your resume, dressing neatly, and acting professionally during job interviews. Don't limit yourself when job-hunting; make a point of applying for as many jobs as possible, and of actively demonstrating your enthusiasm and competence for the various positions. Do your homework thoroughly on each organization you apply to, and use what you've learned about the organization to impress your interviewer with your knowledge and skills. Take the time to learn about the organization's goals—and you'll be well on your way to the career you deserve.

Appendix B: Resources

Resources

Books on nonprofit careers and job-hunting

Following are some of the best books for helpful hints and guidance for finding a job in the nonprofit sector:

Cohen, Lilly, and Young, Dennis R: *Careers for Dreamers and Doers: A Guide to Management Careers in the Nonprofit Sector.* New York: The Foundation Center, 1989.

Everett, Melissa: *Making a Living While Making a Difference: A Guide to Creating Careers With a Conscience.* New York: Bantam Books, 1995.

Krannich, Ronald L., and Krannich, Caryl Rae: *Jobs and Careers with Nonprofit Organizations.* Manassas Park, VA: Impact Publications, 1996.

Lauber, Daniel: *Nonprofits' Job Finder*, 3rd Ed. Rain Forest, IL: Planning/Communications, 1994.

Lewis, William, and Milano, Carol: *Profitable Careers in Nonprofit.* New York: Wiley and Sons, 1987.

Smith, Devon, (ed.): *Great Careers: The Fourth of July Guide to Careers, Internships, and Volunteer Opportunitites in the Nonprofit Sector.* Garrett Park, MD: Garrett Park Press, 1990.

Recommended books on job hunting

Whether you are entering the nonprofit or the private sector, you still need to prepare yourself with good job-hunting skills. The following books provide great guidance on everything from resumés to interviews:

Bolles, Richard Nelson: *What Color is Your Parachute? A Practical Manual for Job-Hunters and Career-Changers.* Updated annually. Berkeley: Ten Speed Press.

Farr, Michael J. *Getting the Job You Really Want.* Indianapolis: JIST Works, 1995.

Farr, Michael J. *How to Get a Job Now!* Indianapolis: JIST Works, 1997.

Figler, Howard: *The Complete Job-Search Handbook.* New York: Henry Holt and Company, Inc., 1988.

French, Albert L. *How to Locate Jobs and Land Interviews.* Hawthorne, NJ: The Career Press, 1993.

Messmer, Max. *50 Ways to Get Hired.* New York: W. Morrow, 1994.

O'Brien, Jack: *The Complete Job Search Organizer: How to Get a Great Job-Fast.* 3rd Ed. Washington, DC: Kiplinger/Times Business, 1997.

Books on Networking

Beatty Richard H. *Richard Beatty's Job Search Networking.* Holbrook, MA: B. Adams, 1994.

Lipnack, Jessica, and Stamps, Jeffrey: *Networking: The First Report and Directory.* New York: Doubleday, 1982.

Lipnack, Jessica, and Stamps, Jeffrey: *The Networking Book: People Connecting With People.* New York: Routledge and Paul, 1986.

Directories

You may check your local library for availability of the following recommended directories, or write to the publisher to obtain a copy.

General Directories:

National Directory of Nonprofit Organizations. Rockville, MD: The Taft Group. Published biannually, this directory lists nonprofit organizations with annual revenues of $100,000 or more. This is an invaluable resource, especially if you want to focus your search on a particular area (i.e., environmental or social welfare causes).

Encyclopedia of Associations and National Organizations. Detroit, MI: Gale Research, Inc. A superb resource. It is updated annually and can probably be found in your local library.

National Trade and Professional Associations. Washington, DC: Columbia Books. This annual directory provides detailed information on 7,500 trade and professional organizations.

National Directory of Addresses and Telephone Numbers. Detroit, MI: Omnigraphics. The ultimate telephone directory for job seekers in any sector, with more than 136,000 listings organized alphabetically. Updated periodically.

Compensation in Nonprofit Organizations. Crete, IL: Abbott, Langer & Associates. Phone: (708) 672-4200. This annual survey provides invaluable information on salaries for over 40,000 positions in more than 2,000 nonprofit organizations, covering 87 job categories.

Directory of Executive Recruiters. Fitzsummon, NH: Kennedy Publications. Many executive recruiters conduct searches on behalf of major nonprofit organizations. This annual directory can be a very helpful tool.

Research Centers Directory. Detroit, MI: Gale Research. A biannual directory that describes over 13,000 nonprofit research units in numerous fields.

Finding a Job in the Nonprofit Sector. Washington, DC: The Taft Group, 1991. This directory offers profiles on almost 1,000 nonprofit organizations. Although there are no plans to update, it is still a helpful reference.

Good Works: A Guide to Careers in Social Change. Colvin, Donna, Ed. New York: Barricade Books, 1994. Profiles over 1,000 nonprofit organizations in the area of social change.

Job Hotlines USA. Harleysville, PA: Career Communications, Inc., 1995. With over 2,000 job hotlines, this is a great resource for telephone numbers that lead to jobs in all fields, nonprofits included.

USAID Current Technical Service Contracts and Grants
USAID, Support Division
Office of Procurement
1100 Wilson, 14th Floor
Rosslyn, VA 20523
Phone: (703) 875-1270

Information on nonprofit organizations funded by the federal government.

The Foundation Directory (Updated annually)
Foundation Center of New York
79 5th Avenue
New York, NY 10003-3076

Summarizes information on over 6,300 foundations.

Public Interest Profiles
The Foundation for Public Affairs
Department R71
P.O. Box 7816
300 Raritan Center Parkway,
Edison, NJ 08818
Phone: (908) 225-1900

The Grant Seeker's Guide (3rd edition, 1989)
  Shellow, Jill R., and Stella, Nancy C., Eds.
  Moyer Bell Limited
  Colonial Hill/RFD 1
  Mount Kisco, NY 10549

The NAPIL Fellowship Guide
  National Association for Public Interest Law
  1666 Connecticut Avenue, NW, Suite 424
  Washington, DC 20009
  Phone: (202) 462-0120

NASCO Guide to Cooperative Careers
  Pederson, Sharon, Ed.
  North American Students of Cooperation
  P.O. Box 7715
  Ann Arbor, MI 48107
  Phone: (313) 663-0889

Internship Opportunities:

The National Directory of Internships (Updated periodically)
  Butterworth Amy S, and Migliore, Sally A., Eds.
  Published by the National Society for Experiential Education
  3509 Haworth Drive, Suite 207
  Raleigh, NC 27609
  Phone: (919) 787-3263

  Listing opportunities for college, graduate, and high school students
  in 61 fields.

NAPIL Directory of Public Interest Legal Internships (Updated period-
  ically)
  Beresovski, Catherine
  Published by the National Association for Public Interest Law
  1666 Connecticut Avenue, NW, Suite 424
  Washington, DC 20009
  Phone: (202) 462-0120

  Employer information on over 150 organizations.

Volunteer Opportunities:

Alternatives to the Peace Corps: A Directory of Third World and U.S. Volunteer Opportunities (Updated periodically)
Published by the Institute for Food and Development Policy
398 60th Street
Oakland, CA 94103
Phone: (510) 864-4400

Volunteerism: The Directory of Organizations, Training, Programs and Publications
Harriet Clyde Kipps, Ed.
Published by R.R. Bowker
245 West 17th Street
New York, NY 10011
Phone: (800) 521-8110

Looking to work abroad? Many opportunities exist in the international arena and are detailed in numerous directories, including: *The Almanac of International Jobs and Careers; Amerrican Jobs Abroad; Guide to Careers in World Affairs*; and *The Nonprofit's Job Finder.* You can locate these and other directories through your local library. See also Newspapers/Periodicals.

Newspapers/Periodicals

There are several periodicals, usually published on a monthly basis, that provide valuable information on the nonprofit market, as well as listings of job opportunities. The following are highly recommended:

Community Jobs
Published by: ACCESS: Networking in the Public Interest
30 Irving Place, 9th Floor
New York, NY 10003
Phone: (212) 475-1001

This national nonprofit employment newspaper is published monthly, and usually lists anywhere from 250 to 300 jobs in the nonprofit sector each month.

Chronicle of Philanthropy
1255 23rd Street, NW
Washington, DC 20037
Phone: (800) 728-2819

This bi-weekly newspaper also has an on-line edition (see Internet Resources).

Philanthropy Journal
Published by Nonprofit Books
5 West Hargett Street, Suite 805
Raleigh, NC 27601

See Internet Resources for information on the on-line edition of this monthly journal.

The Non-Profit Times
Davis Information Group
190 Tamarack Cr.
Skillman, NJ 08558
Phone: (609) 921-1251

A monthly journal that includes up to 30 job listings in the nonprofit sector.

Association Trends

7910 Woodmont Avenue, #1150
Bethesda, MD 20814-3062
Phone: (301) 652-8666

This weekly newspaper provides useful information on associations as well as numerous job postings and a job referral service.

National Business Employment Weekly

P.O. Box 435
Chicopee, MA 01021-0435
Phone: (800) 562-4868

The first and third issues of each month contain a special section with 40-plus ads for professionals in the nonprofit sector.

Opportunities in Public Interest Law

Published by: ACCESS: Networking in the Public Interest
50 Beacon Street
Boston, MA 02108
Phone: (617) 720-JOBS

Published twice a year, this bulletin lists current jobs and internships in nonprofit and government public interest law organizations.

Opportunity NOCs

The Management Center
870 Market Street, Suite 800
San Francisco, CA 94102
Phone: (415) 362-9735

NOCs stands for Nonprofit Organizations Classified. This weekly newspaper focuses on San Francisco Bay Area nonprofit job opportunities, and provides information on workshops and services for nonprofit agencies. It also lists Internet sites covering different areas of the U.S.

Public Interest Employment Report

Public Interest Clearinghouse
200 McAllister Street
San Francisco, CA 94102-4978
Phone: (415) 255-1714

This newsletter focuses on California and the West. It is published twice a month and lists up to 75 social change jobs in each issue.

City Limits

This monthly newspaper advertises nonprofit positions in the New York City area. For information, telephone: (212) 925-9820.

Foundation News & Commentary

Publishes articles of general interest and occasional ads for jobs. For information, telephone: (800) 544-0155.

Nonprofit Times

A monthly newspaper that primarily advertises fund-raising positions. For information, telephone: (609) 921-1251.

International Career Employment Opportunities

A biweekly journal that lists more than 500 job openings in the U.S. and abroad, including nonprofit organizations. For information, telephone: (804) 985-6444 or Fax: (804) 985-6828.

Referral Centers

These organizations are good sources for obtaining information and leads on various aspects of job-hunting in the nonprofit sector:

Enterprise, Inc.
    2160 W. Charleston, Suite L345,
    Las Vegas, NV 89102
    Phone: (702) 259-6570
    Fax: (702) 259-0244
    E-mail: info@nonprofitjobs.org
    Web site: http://www.nonprofitjobs.org/

    Their on-line service is the Community Career Center (see Internet Resources).

Nonprofit Career Network
    P.O. Box 2243
    Middletown, CT 06457
    Phone: (860) 344-0400
    Fax: (860) 704-0730
    E-mail: info-request@nonprofitcareer.com
    Web site: http://www.nonprofitcareer.com/

ACCESS: Networking in the Public Interest
    50 Beacon Street
    Boston, MA 02108
    Phone: (617) 720-JOBS

    For a fee, this organization will perform searches for job hunters in 100 different nonprofit areas. Also provides descriptions of nonprofit organizations.

Volunteer: The National Center
    1111 North 19 Street, Suite 500
    Arlington, VA 22209
    Phone: (703) 276-0542

    This center provides referrals to over 100 volunteer clearinghouses across the country.

The Environmental Careers Organization
179 South Street
Boston, MA 02110
Phone: (617) 426-4375

Provides information and referrals to jobs, internships, and volunteer opportunities in the environmental field.

Job Bank USA
1420 Spring Hill Road, Suite 480
McLean, VA 22102
Phone: (800) 291-1USA
Fax: (703) 847-1494

This is one of the leading job banks in the country. Membership fee required.

Associations

Professional associations provide a great networking opportunity within the nonprofit world, as well as information on particular organizations. Many associations publish their own newsletters, which can not only provide valuable information but may also have job postings. Your local library will have directories for the thousands of associations you can tap for information and contacts, including organizations that might focus on an area of particular interest to you. Here are a few I recommend:

National Society for Fund Raising Executives (NSFRE)
    1101 King Street, Suite 700
    Alexandria, VA 22314
    Phone: (800) 666-FUND or (703) 684-0410
    Fax: (703) 684-0540
    E-mail: nsfre@nsfre.org
    Web site: http://www.nsfre.org/

    This association is particularly useful for information and guidance on fund-raising for nonprofit organizations. Publishes *ESS Employment Opportunities Newsletter*.

Society for Nonprofit Organizations
    6314 Odana Road, Suite 1
    Madison, WI 53719
    (608) 274-9777

National Council of Nonprofit Organizations
    1001 Connecticut Avenue, NW, Suite 900
    Washington, DC 20036
    Phone: (202) 833-5740

Association for Research on Nonprofit Organizations and
    Voluntary Action
    c/o Barbara Long
    Route 2, Box 696
    Pullman, WA 99163
    (509) 332-3417

National Association for Public Interest Law (NAPIL)
  1118 22nd Street, NW, Third Floor
  Washington, DC 20037
  Phone: (202) 466-3686

Council on Foundations
  1828 L Street, NW, Suite 300
  Washington, DC 20036
  Phone: (202) 466-6512

Nonprofit Management Association
  315 W 9th Street, Suite 1100
  Los Angeles, CA 90015
  (213) 623-7080

Nonprofit Marketing Forum
  3707 Military Road, NW
  Washington, DC 20015
  (202) 244-7256

National Center for Nonprofit Boards
  2000 L Street, NW, Suite 411
  Washington, DC 20036
  (202) 452-6262

Nonprofits Mailers Federation
  815 15th Street, NW
  Washington, DC 20017-1094
  (202) 628-4380

National Network of Grantmakers
  666 Broadway, Room 520
  New York, NY 10012
  (619) 220-0690

Internet Resources

Countless Internet resources offer everything from career guidance for the nonprofit sector to job postings throughout the country. Following are just a few sites on the World Wide Web that will be useful to your search:

Nonprofit Career Network
http://www.nonprofitcareer.com/

This is one of the best sites for getting information or assistance on just about every aspect of your search. In addition to job postings, you will find a Resource Center, information on job fairs, conferences, workshops, conventions, and volunteer opportunities, directories for nonprofit organizations and professional services, and answers to frequently asked questions.

Internet Nonprofit Center
http://www.nonprofits.org/

You will find numerous helpful resources here, including a library of data about the nonprofit sector and its organizations, a Nonprofit Locator to help you find any charity in the U.S., information on nonprofit corporations from the companies themselves, volunteer opportunities, a chat corner, and other resources.

Community Career Center
http://www.nonprofitjobs.org/

This site is run by Enterprise, Inc. (see Referral Centers), with the aim of matching job-seekers with nonprofit employers. The site includes job postings, candidate profiles, resource links, and member services.

Good Works
http://www.essential.org/goodworks/

A great resource for learning more about the nonprofit sector. This site provides pertinent data, including aims and projects, for over 1,000 social change organizations, as well as a jobs search guide.

Philanthropy Journal Online
http://www.pj.org/

This is one of the most useful sites you can find for information on non-profit organizations, current trends, and links to job opportunities.

Chronicle of Philanthropy
http://philanthropy.com/

This site also contains numerous helpful articles on the nonprofit sector, as well as job postings.

GuideStar
http://www.guidestar.org/

Numerous articles, tips, and resources for donors and volunteers, as well as a news service and classified ads.

Career Web
http://www.careerweb.com/

Helpful information on how to organize a job search.

Opportunity NOCs
http://www.opnocs.org/

This site is primarily focused on the New England area, but there are links to other areas throughout the country. It includes job listings and information on volunteer and internship opportunities.

Action Without Borders
http://www.idealist.org/

This site provides information on organizations, volunteer and internship opportunities, programs and services, and job listings in 120 countries worldwide.

Volunteer Center
http://www.volunteercenter.org/

Focusing primarily on Orange County, California, this site includes both volunteer and paid opportunities in a number of different areas, along with a nonprofit resource center.

Townonline.com/Working
http://www.townonline.com/

This site's focus is on eastern Massachusetts. It provides opportunities for job hunters and employers to post profiles and find the ideal match.

Appendix C:
Index

The 100 Best Nonprofits to Work for – by Category

Art-related Missions
Guggenheim Museum / 103
Isabella Stewart Gardner Museum / 121
Metropolitan Museum of Art / 142
Museum of Contemporary Art / 146
Museum of Fine Arts, Boston / 149
Whitney Museum of Art / 236

Aviation-related Missions
Confederate Air Force / 77
Experimental Aircraft Association / 93

Education-related Missions
The Children's Museum of Boston / 62
Close Up Foundation / 71
Colonial Williamsburg Foundation, Inc. / 74
Consumers Union / 79
Harvard University / 108
Museum of Science / 151
Museum of Television and Radio / 154
Mystic Seaport Museum / 156
National Baseball Hall of Fame / 165
Outward Bound / 186
The League of Women Voters / 130
The Network, Inc. / 180
WGBH Educational Foundation / 233
World Game Institute / 240

Environment-related Missions

Health-related Missions

Human Rights Missions
Amnesty International, USA / 28
Human Rights Watch / 110

Issue or Constituent Advocacy/Social Change Missions
American Association of Retired Persons / 9
American Civil Liberties Union / 12
Center for Science in the Public Interest / 50
The Hemlock Society / 114
The Massachusetts Public Interest Research Group / 140
National Association for the Advancement of Colored People / 159
National Organization for Women / 168
National Rifle Association / 170
Ohio Citizen Action / 184
People for the Ethical Treatment of Animals / 190
Union of Concerned Scientists / 218
Western States Center / 231
Zero Population Growth / 245

Philanthropic Missions
Henry J. Kaiser Family Foundation / 116
United Negro College Fund / 220
United Way of America / 222
W. Alton Jones Foundation, Inc. / 229

Relief Missions
American Red Cross / 20
International Rescue Committee / 118

Research Missions

Social Service Missions

Zoos and Aquariums

About the Authors

Leslie Hamilton and Robert Tragert are a husband-and-wife writing and researching team. They make their home in the suburban Boston area.

Ms. Hamilton is the author of *The Cheapskate's Guide to Living Cheaper and Better* (Carol Publishing) and *365 Four-Star Videos You (Probably) Haven't Seen* (Contemporary Books). Mr. Tragert's research includes activities in environmental and regulatory areas; he has worked as an environmental engineer and safety and readiness expert in a variety of settings.